GREEN HILLS *and* BLUE LAGOONS

A Peace Corps Memoir

JOHN PENISTEN

TABLE OF CONTENTS

FOREWORD

This is a series of reflections and reminiscences of life as a U.S. Peace Corps Volunteer in the Fiji Islands, South Pacific, in 1968-69. These sketches describe the experiences, difficulties, and rewards of earning one's living in a foreign culture where one must learn to speak the language, follow the customs, and adopt the lifestyle of the local people in order to survive.

The text relates the adventures of three young Americans, fresh out of college and filled with youthful idealism, and how they came to be on an island called Vanua Levu, the "Big Land," in Fiji.

These three young men (the author is one of them), with varied backgrounds from different parts of the United States, came together for this one period in their lives. Far from their respective roots, they learned and shared much, about themselves and with others in a communal culture.

These stories are true and accurate accounts of real experiences and adventures. They attempt to share the successes and failures, the joys and sorrows, the good and bad, as these young Americans break the cultural barriers around them and become immersed in a totally different culture.

These stories reflect their dedication and resolve and their adoption and acceptance into the Fijian culture and society into which they were placed. This is the story of what they accomplished and gained as U.S. Peace Corps Volunteers in the small island country of Fiji in the South Pacific.

ACKNOWLEDGEMENTS

Thanks to the wonderful people of Fiji and especially the people of Cakaudrove Province for allowing us to live among them for two years. Through them, we came to understand and know the real Fiji. And in the process, we learned much about ourselves as well. Without them, none of this would have been possible.

I want to thank my two closest friends and fellow Volunteers, Charles Matthews and David Reed for being there with me. They are the best friends a man could want. Without them, the entire experience would not have been the same.

Much of the material is from the journal I kept during my time in Fiji and my own reminiscences. Some material and anecdotal information came from conversations and resources provided over the years by my good friends, Charlie and Dave. And while these adventures took place over 50 years ago, I'm sure that Charlie and Dave would agree that it seems like only yesterday.

I've often told others over the years that while I have a college degree, I got my real education in the Peace Corps.

John Penisten
Hilo, Hawaii
2020

DEDICATION

For the people of Cakaudrove Province, Fiji.

PRONUNCIATION KEY

The Fijian language was first put into written form in the 1830's by the early missionaries in the islands. A phonetic system was used to make spelling of words as easy as possible. The system of pronunciation evolved as follows:

B is MB as in number – Bau is pronounced Mbau

C is TH as in that – Cakaudrove is pronounced Thakaundrove

D is ND as in end – Nadi is pronounced Nandi

G is NG as in sing – Koronatoga is pronounced Koronatonga

Q is NGG as in younger – Qelelevu is pronounced Nggelelevu

CHAPTER 1

THE BEGINNING – HAWAI`I

*P*eace Corps Goes to Paradise! So read the recruiting poster in big bold letters. The poster featured a dazzling full color picture of a beautiful blue lagoon surrounded by white sand beaches and towering palm trees. On a cold February day in Des Moines, Iowa, it was a truly exotic scene. It was something straight out of "Tales of the South Pacific," and it was captivating. The Peace Corps was planning to send Volunteers to Samoa and other islands of the South Pacific.

Wow! The South Pacific I thought: beautiful white sand beaches, coral reefs, swaying palm trees, and beautiful island maidens. Of course, all the usual false stereotypes were conjured up in my youthful imagination. I remember saying to myself at the time, "Now that's for me!" Little did I know at the time that that poster was the beginning of my own personal adventure.

"Would you believe this lousy rain Dave? They never told us about this part of training," I stated as we struggled to squeeze under the flimsy paper umbrella.

"Good grief," he said, "this is incredible. I've never seen it rain this hard before!"

"Well, we're halfway there, so we might as well keep going," I said.

We were at the bottom of the gulch now and crossing the bridge. A raging river swept along under the bridge. The road continued up the side of the steep rain forested ravine. The schoolhouse where we had our language classes was just beyond the top.

"My God, we're going to be soaked before we get there," Dave said over the roar of the river and rain.

"Yeah, and we'll probably catch a cold sitting around all day in wet clothes too," I replied gloomily.

Such was the life of a lowly Peace Corps trainee. It had its miserable moments, maybe too many of them. On this morning in the fall of 1967, we were among some 75 Volunteer trainees heading for John M. Ross School near Ninole, Hawai`i. It was pouring down rain as usual. The Hamakua Coast of the Big Island of Hawai`i is well known for its tropical rainstorms.

We had arrived in Hawai'i on October 23, 1967, as the trainee program for Fiji I, the first ever Peace Corps group bound for Fiji. We were housed in a dilapidated old sugar plantation village called Honohina. It was about a mile down the road from the former village school where we attended our language and culture classes and had our meals in the cafeteria.

In August, I graduated with a liberal arts degree from Drake University in Des Moines, Iowa, my hometown. Upon return from a short vacation trip, I found a big envelope from Peace Corps-Washington waiting in the mail. I had applied to join the Peace Corps the previous spring. All through the summer I heard nothing.

I left on my vacation trip wondering just what I would do when I got back home, as I had not really made any other plans. I really was not sure what I wanted to do with my life at that point. So, the Peace

Corps still seemed to be an attractive alternative. It would get me out of Iowa and give me a chance to see some exotic places and to do something different.

I had originally applied to join the Samoa Peace Corps program. And then I opened the envelope and read: "Congratulations. You are invited to join a Peace Corps training program for the Fiji Islands. The training site will be in Hawai`i. The program will begin October 17, 1967."

Wow! Fiji! Where in the heck is Fiji? I had not the slightest idea. I think I had heard of it before, but I was not sure. As I looked at a world atlas, I discovered that Fiji was almost next door to Samoa in the far-away South Pacific.

Although I had signed up for Samoa, it did not seem too bad an idea to be going to Fiji, I reasoned. It was in the South Pacific and that is where I really wanted to go. Plus, it was the first program in Fiji. That should make it an even more interesting experience.

The fact that the training site would be in Hawai`i was as much an influence in my accepting the invitation as anything. I completed the necessary paperwork and returned them to Peace Corps-Washington as soon as possible.

During the next few weeks, I gathered my gear, read a lot on Fiji and the South Pacific, and put my affairs in order. On October 17, 1967, I said farewell to my parents, who though sad to see me go, were enthusiastic about my joining the Peace Corps. My mother fretted, as all mothers are prone to do, as she said, "Take care of yourself and please write to us." And my father added, "Let us know if we can be of any help."

I hugged them both and stepped onto a United Airlines DC-6 prop plane for my very first airplane ride, a 30-minute hop to Omaha. I continued to San Francisco to the staging site which the Peace Corps had arranged for us.

On the flight to San Francisco, I met another Iowan who was joining the Samoa program, also training in Hawai`i. When we arrived in San Francisco, we ended up rooming together in a grubby old YMCA hotel in downtown which Peace Corps put us in.

We spent four days in San Francisco, mainly to attend a series of meetings relative to training, to complete medical checks, and so on. We were also duly fingerprinted, photographed, and probably filed for life in the bureaucratic bowels of the U.S. government.

We left San Francisco for Hilo, Hawai`i, on October 23, 1967. We flew on United Airlines direct to Hilo and arrived at mid-day. Waiting to greet us at the airport were the Fijian and Indian language and cultural instructors who would be working with us in the training program. They gave us a super welcome complete with dances and songs of Fiji and really got Fiji I off to a great start.

From Hilo, we were taken by bus up the Hamakua Coast some 15 miles to the village of Honohina. The idea of seeing beautiful lush green Hawai`i in October was a real contrast for a kid from Iowa. Having never seen palm trees or banana plants or any tropical foliage, I was entranced by the sheer verdant beauty of the landscape of sugar cane fields and rain forest as our bus rolled up the Big Island coast.

This was to be our home for the next 12 weeks. We were split up into groups of 10 or 12 and assigned to cottages. These were old clapboard wood frame houses that were 30-40 years old at least. In typical Hawaiian plantation style, they were painted a dull green with red corrugated iron roofs.

Over the next several days, we settled in, became familiar with our surroundings, and began a routine of daily language and culture classes. I developed a friendship with a thin dark-haired guy named Dave Reed. Dave was a serious individual, who sincerity was beyond any doubt. He had a need to prove himself which he continually did with hard work and perseverance. One thing for sure, Dave was a hell of a nice guy and we became close friends during training and after.

Dave, from Silver Springs, Maryland, was a recent graduate of the University of Maryland. Like me, he earned a liberal arts degree. He had ended up in the Fiji I program by mistake in fact. He had originally joined the Peace Corps with the idea of going to Micronesia in the North Pacific. There were mix-ups or something, perhaps a program cancellation, so Dave was offered the Fiji I program and accepted.

Something similar happened to Charles Matthews. He got into Fiji I by way of a program cancellation. He had almost completed training for India when the program was abruptly cancelled due to political problems in India at the time. Charlie was offered the Fiji I program instead and accepted. He was from Chicago, Illinois, and a recent liberal arts graduate from Roosevelt University there.

Charlie was a fast-talking, quick-witted fellow with a wonderful sense of humor. He was intelligent, energetic, and a good listener. Charlie had the ability to be a friend. He was able to tune in to others very readily. He was the type of person who others sought out and could have confidence in. He also liked to have a good time.

I got to know Charlie well enough in training to admire his intelligence, skill with the Fijian language, and his general good-natured self. We would become the best of friends before we were through the next two years.

The training program itself was an intensive 12 long weeks. It included days that started at 7:30 a.m. and ended at 4:30 p.m., with an hour lunch break. We then had an evening session or class that lasted a couple of more hours. Most of the hours were spent with our language instructors in monotonous dull drill and more drill and repetition on the language. Other classes dealt with culture and the history of Fiji as well as within our areas of specialty.

Our trainee group consisted of potential teachers, co-operative or-ganizers, and agriculture extension workers. I happened to fit into the latter category, as did Dave and Charlie. The training attempted to give us a quick course in tropical agriculture. Given the fact that we were liberal arts grads, it was somewhat of an unrealistic notion that we could become competent agriculturists in 12 weeks. But we tried.

Training was a grueling experience. It was basically a weeding out process. It attempted to weed out those trainees who, for one reason or another, were deemed unable to make it in Fiji. Whether the selection process was fair or practical is another question.

A decision on whether a trainee was finally selected was a combi-nation of an overall assessment. Into this decision went his/her prog-ress in language training, demonstrated specialty skill, evaluations of instructors and staff, peer evaluations, and evaluations by psycholo-gists or "shrinks" as we referred to them.

Training was geared to make or break a trainee. Perhaps it was just as well too. Compared to Hawai'i, Fiji was an undeveloped coun-try. One of the toughest parts of training for us was a three-week campout in the Waipio Valley on the Big Island of Hawai`i. It was in Waipio that we got our jungle survival training and learned some new agricultural techniques. With the very primitive conditions un-der which we lived in Waipio, we figured that even Fiji would have to be better. It was.

By early January 1968, our training program was entering the last phase. From an initial trainee group of some 75, the deselection process and personal decisions to quit had reduced our group to around 60. At the final selection process, 56 of us were selected and sworn in as U.S. Peace Corps Volunteers.

I remember that we were called in individually that day and told by an instructor that we were going to Fiji or not. I was called in by one of the instructors and told I had been selected.

Wow! I made it. I am going to Fiji! I was very happy and relieved at the same time. The pressure and tension that had been building up to this day was pretty severe. Those of us who were selected were quite happy and yet felt a tinge of sadness when we learned of the quick departure of a couple of our friends who did not make it.

From the Big Island of Hawai`i, we flew to Honolulu on January 15, 1968. We would have a couple of days of rest and relaxation in Honolulu before departing for Fiji.

CHAPTER 2

BULA FIJI!

As our World Airways charter flight roared down the runway at Honolulu on takeoff for Fiji, our group's spirits soared. Because of the wonderful relationship with our Fijian and Indian language training instructors, each Fiji I Volunteer had a high sense of camaraderie, morale, and esprit de corps. Our time had come, and we were ready for it. We were Fiji bound.

Collectively we were one, with a singular idealistic purpose of going to Fiji to do our best. My very first journal entry describes my feelings at the time:

January 18, 1968 – The Beginning

"Well, I am undertaking what I hope to be a great adventure—two years as a Peace Corps Volunteer in the islands of Fiji. After twelve weeks of training in Hawai`i, language and agriculture, I am now prepared to attempt to do a good job for my country, the Peace Corps, and the people of Fiji."

I think it fair to state that this attitude permeated our entire group. The positive feelings we all shared toward our common experiences and anticipated future in Fiji carried us through our training program. This spirit would now help carry us through the initial apprehension of arrival in country.

The charter jet that carried us to Fiji was shared by another Peace Corps group bound for Samoa. Since Pago Pago, American Samoa, is on the way to Fiji from Hawai`i, the plane landed at Pago Pago International Airport in the early morning hours of January 19, 1968.

The Samoan Peace Corps group had also just completed training in Hawai`i, on the island of Molokai. I knew a couple of people in this group, as we had initially met in San Francisco. I also renewed acquaintance with the one fellow from Iowa and wished him luck.

After a lusty exchange of farewell songs by both groups of volunteers, Fiji I boarded the plane. The next stop was Nadi International Airport on the island of Viti Levu, a little more than an hour's flight from Samoa.

Our first glimpse of Fiji was from about 30,000 ft. as we flew over parts of Vanua Levu and Viti Levu, the two largest islands. Peering down through the thick cumulus clouds, in the early morning sun, the first sight of our new home was thrilling.

We knew definitely that we had arrived when the flight attendant announced, "We have landed at Nadi International Airport. We would like to welcome you to your new home and wish you the best of luck." With that, we exited into a brilliant sunny Fijian morning, left behind our past, and entered our future.

The Fiji Islands number some 700 large volcanic mountainous islands and small coral atolls. They cover an area of some 100,000 square miles and straddle the 180th. Meridian, the International Date Line. Viti Levu is the largest island with some 4,000 square miles, and Vanua Levu is the second largest island in size with about 2,000 square miles of land. Suva, the capital, has a population of some 93,000 (2017 data) and is in southeastern Viti Levu. The entire population of Fiji numbers 884,000 (2017 data). Data from 2012 indicated there are 511,000 native Fijians and 290,000 are Indo-Fijians with the remainder being composed of various other ethnic groups.

Nadi International Airport is not large compared to other major airports, but for a small island country like Fiji it is adequate. Our arrival brought out a few curious locals hoping for a chance to see what the new "kai Merekes" (the Americans) looked like.

We spent some time getting our luggage through customs. Afterwards, it was on to the nearby Mocambo Hotel for rest and relaxation after the long flight. We had to lay over in Nadi for a while as only part of our group at a time could fly to Suva, the capital. The local airline, Fiji Airways, was using an old DC-3 to shuttle us on the half-hour flight to Suva on the other side of Viti Levu.

We spent a few pleasant hours breakfasting, sunning, and even swimming in the hotel pool. We even tried out our skill at speaking Fijian with the hotel workers, to their utter amusement and delight.

Initially, the Fijians would assume we were expert at speaking their language and would rapid fire questions and conversation at us. Befuddled but brave, we would attempt an answer and no matter how bad it came out the Fijians would express pure delight at our efforts. "Sa matai na vosa vaka Viti!" (You are so smart at speaking Fijian) was often heard.

By the afternoon of our arrival day, the entire group had flown to Nausori Airport just outside the capital of Suva. We were then taken by bus to Nasinu Teachers Training College on the outskirts of the city.

Nasinu was our first real stopping place in Fiji. Our group got a chance to catch its collective breath here for a few days of rest and familiarization with new surroundings. We were put up in old barracks type housing that normally served as a dormitory for teacher trainees. It was here that we got a first taste of local foods at the dining hall.

Nasinu was a transition for us, a place where we got an orientation to Fiji. General informational meetings were held and we were given our first monetary allowances and got to meet our Peace Corps director and staff. They had already been in country for a while preparing for our arrival.

Nasinu was a the jumping off place for our introduction to Fiji in the raw. And what better introduction could we have gotten than an official welcome by the then Chief Minister, Ratu Sir Kamesese Mara, Fiji's esteemed political leader.

Ratu Mara as head of Fiji's government visited us one afternoon soon after our arrival. Ratu Mara was strongly pro-American and very much pro-Peace Corps. He no doubt had a lot to do with officially inviting the Peace Corps into Fiji in the first place.

With this in mind, Mara came to give us an official welcome. As it turned out, Fiji I welcomed him into the hall at Nasinu that day. We gave him a rousing rendition of the Fijian call to arms song, <u>Rogo Mai,</u> commemorating the famed Fiji Battalion of World War II fame. We had learned to sing this revered song in our Hawai`i training program.

Ratu Mara was completely overcome by the occasion and said in his remarks to us, "I came here to welcome you to Fiji, but instead you have welcomed me." The absolutely positive feelings generated by this event sealed our good relationship and certainly put our presence in Fiji off to a good start. After Mara's talk with us, he went down the line and shook our hands with a personal message of gratitude thanking us for coming to Fiji. Afterwards, there was a general feeling of elation throughout our group.

The next few days were filled with various orientation talks, meetings, and gatherings with various government officials. During this period we also had free time to ourselves which we used to explore the capital, Suva.

My journal entry for January 20, 1968, notes:

"...also went into Suva for the first time today, for a couple of hours. It is a real thrill to experience for the first time a foreign land and its people. The Suva open market is just like one always sees in the movies and reads about...really a thrill to see these things alive and as they really are..."

Suva is an old British colonial city. At the same time it is a city of the South Pacific with a unique flavor and atmosphere. After arriving at the Peace Corps headquarters office just above downtown Suva, most of the Volunteers walked on down into the city to explore.

The sights were marvelous to the young American eyes. The narrow streets, buzzing traffic, and people everywhere crowding the walkways and stores made for long-lasting first impressions. Buying, bartering, barking and a chattering confusion of languages foreign to the ear were evident. Smells, odors, and stenches abounded, like the sweet heavy aroma of copra (dried coconut) ready for market, the piquant fragrance of curry powder and spices, and the mixed scents emanating from shops, cafes, milk bars, sewers, canals, drain ditches all created a multitudinous assault on the senses. There was so much that was different and new.

The stores and shops of downtown Suva are packed tightly together. The Indian shopkeepers sell a variety of goods from general merchandise to duty-free electronics, cameras, and more. The Indians are aggressive competitors and will even stop you on the street to hawk their wares.

One of the biggest attractions of Suva is the Suva Market, a large open air marketplace located near the Suva harbor waterfront. The market is a fantasyland of the sights, sounds, and smells that typify this South Pacific island nation. Here you can experience the all the multi-cultural diversity, flavors, foods, and colors that represent Fiji.

Fijian women selling their woven mats, hats, fans, and baskets, as well as sea shells and trinkets, were everywhere. Indian peddlers were selling special delicacies, candies, fruits and drinks from street carts. And in the main marketplace you can buy foodstuffs from fresh fish to local fruits and vegetables to live chickens and pigs. It's a somewhat chaotic scene accented by the color, smells and noise of the place. It all adds up to a splendid display of organized confusion to the newcomer. There certainly wasn't anything like this in Iowa!

Along with getting acquainted with the surroundings we were also introduced to what the city had to offer otherwise. We had heard quite a lot about Fiji Beer, brewed locally in Suva. The brew came only in large quart bottles and carried a pretty strong kick. The alcoholic content was about 9% compared to American beer which was usually about 3.2%. To the unaccustomed young American, a couple of bottles of Fiji Bitter were more than enough to get high on. More than that left one totally devastated.

Toward the end of our five day stay at Nasinu, most of us were informed of our specific job assignment and location and the date we would be leaving for it. Many of the teacher volunteers had already left for their respective assignments.

The January 22, 1968, journal entry notes:

"...our job assignments were also announced. I am going to be on Vanua Levu. I am not sure where exactly. But they did say each man would live in a village with his own "bure." So, I am very happy indeed about our assignments, though it would be quite adventurous to be on one of the small outer islands."

Little did I know at this point how adventurous my assignment to Vanua Levu would be, perhaps as much if not more so than being placed on a small outer island. I found out soon enough that my assignment would be Buca Bay in Cakaudrove Province on Vanua Levu. I was being assigned to Cakaudrove to work on the agriculture census along with Dave Reed, Charles Matthews, and Paul Korenberg. These fellows were assigned to Savusavu, Natewa Bay, and the island of Taveuni, respectively.

At the Peace Corps Office in Suva, I eagerly sought out the exact location of my post, Buca Bay, on the map. Along with Dave and Charlie, we discovered that our posts would be within fifty miles of each other. Paul Korenberg, on the other hand, was to be across the water on Taveuni Island, a few miles opposite of Buca Bay, my post. Dave, Charlie and I were in the fortunate position of being on mainland Vanua Levu, where we at least had access to town, Savusavu, and more importantly (as it turned out later on) to each other.

Before we could be shipped out to our assignments however, there was one more orientation session for us to attend. This was a brief training sessions on the agriculture census that we were to work on in Vanua Levu.

From Nasinu Teachers Training College we were transferred to the Lami Cooperative Training School on the opposite side of Suva and closer to the city itself. Here the agriculture fellows, about eight of us, and some of the co-operative organizer volunteers were put up for the next week and a half or so.

The first couple of days at Lami were a transition phase again for us. In the Peace Corps, you are always leaving one transition phase and entering another. The Fiji Department of Agriculture, for which we would be working, arranged a couple of field trips for us. Our first was a day trip up the Wainibuka River Valley near Suva to visit a banana harvesting area.

The journal for January 25, 1968, notes:

"...our group took a field trip up the Wainibuka River Valley to observe banana producing areas. Really something to see the villagers float their produce down the river and then pack the bananas at given loading points. It was beautiful country all throughout the area with many hills and much forest. In the evening, we watched the bananas brought in and inspected at the Suva wharf. This also is quite a procedure. Fiji sells bananas only to New Zealand, so their market is quite limited."

Another field trip arranged for us was a visit to Koronivia Agriculture Research Station. This was located outside Suva near Nasinu. Here we saw many different crops grown, plus dairy and hog operations. At least the Agriculture Department was attempting to give us an introduction to Fiji agriculture.

During this stay at Lami, time started to weigh a little heavy on our hands, psychologically and physically. Our training program on the census work did not actually begin for a few days and the daily activities being arranged for us were more or less to just fill the time. At one point, a short lived epidemic broke out among those of us at Lami.

The journal entry for January 27th notes:

"...seems like a virus or flu is breaking out. Three of our guys here have come down with fever and so on in the last twenty-four hours. Hope I don't get it. Don't believe it's real serious though."

At this time, I was still recovering from a broken collar bone sustained in training in Hawai`i. I didn't need another physical affliction at that particular time.

Psychologically, we were being tested as well. Most of us were tired of "barracks" or "dormitory" style living by this time. After twelve weeks of living together during training, and our brief rest vacation in Honolulu, and then more of the same here in Fiji after arriving, well, most of us were ready for a change.

The January 27th journal entry continues:

"...went to a movie in town tonight, it is nice to get away and see something different. This place, Lami, is not the greatest to live in. Though it is clean and comfortable, the meals are the same, no variety. Breakfast is oatmeal, tea, and banana; lunch is roro (taro leaves) and yam; dinner is roro or fish, yam, and dalo (taro root)."

The last days of January, 1968, came rapidly. We finally began our census training which included instruction on how to collect data, fill out the necessary paper work, and how to use and mark the aerial photographs with which we would be working.

The agriculture census was the first major effort in Fiji to gather data on the overall extent of agricultural production and development in the country. It was being jointly sponsored by the Fiji government and the United Nations. Our roles were to be a combination of actual field enumeration of farmers' holdings plus supervision of other census workers in Cakaudrove Province.

Despite all the training we received both in Hawai`i and initially in Fiji in the language, culture, and history of the country, we never really learned how to survive the rigors of what we were soon to encounter in the field. We eventually learned how to survive the rigors of bush living with on-the-job training. Getting by in the bush, in the villages, on our own is something that we had to learn on our own. In this case, experience was the best teacher. We just didn't know it at the time.

The psychological strain was still evident from the January 30, 1968, entry:

"...I am getting more tired of this place where we are staying. I'll be glad when we leave this weekend for Vanua Levu. The change will be for the better I hope."

We were to leave the first weekend in February, 1968, for our assignments. Our departure from Suva would be on the Fijian Princess, an inter-island copra trading ship. We would be sailing direct for Savusavu, the provincial center for Cakaudrove Province. During these last few days in Suva we were busy with our census training, some other related field trips, and generally making last minute shopping trips into Suva. Some of us stocked up on clothing needs like shorts, socks, and footwear as well as things for our living quarters. With great anticipation, we awaited the departure for our assignments.

Along with other last minute things, we managed to find time to visit the hotel bar just down the road from our quarters at Lami. At the time, the Tradewinds Hotel was quite new and offered a nice place for us to spend the evening. It also gave us a chance to break away from the depressing atmosphere of the Lami Co-op Center.

The January 31st entry in the journal notes:

"...visited the hotel bar just down the road from here and had some beer. A Fijian bought a round of beer and expressed his gratitude to us PCV's for coming here to teach and work with his people. This person really did mean this, and I am deeply touched by his expression of gratitude. I hope that I'll be able to live up to the expectations and be able to do a successful job with and for the people of Fiji."

As was to be a story repeated frequently during our stay in Fiji, our boat did not leave as originally planned. This characteristic of Fiji, the apparent inability to stick to a schedule, was to plague us our entire term of service there. For me personally, it was something that took a while to accept. Perhaps the best thing for an American to do upon arrival in the South Pacific is to dispose of first, his watch, and then all predisposition he may have on keeping or meeting schedules and deadlines. In a place like Fiji, one soon learns that there is no concept of time as we know it.

We spent the weekend in Suva making our final preparations and gathering all our gear together. The Fijian Princess was to leave the Suva wharf on Monday, February 5th. We arrived at the wharf in the late afternoon and got checked on board along with our gear. Our Peace Corps Director, John Hurley, some of the other staff, and the three volunteer secretaries, Barb Bukar, Kee Jones and Betty Pyzik, were there to see us off.

We also were met by our boss, James Makasiale, the Agriculture Officer, Cakaudrove Province. "Big James," as he was known, was over six feet tall and easily weighed 250 lbs. He was a recent graduate of the University of Hawai'i, School of Tropical Agriculture. James had a personality, friendliness, and a heart that matched the rest of his ample dimensions. His easy going demeanor allowed us to be at ease right away. He had a natural liking for others and especially for us as Americans and as Peace Corps Volunteers. Even though James was a native of Lau in eastern Fiji, he was also an American, at least in heart. We couldn't have gotten a better boss and friend that Big James.

Dave Reed recalled later about James, noting his first impression upon meeting James at the Suva wharf was really positive. Dave felt that James was a really nice guy and that he was going to help us out as we got into our job assignments. As Dave noted, he was a friend who really knew the place and that "he had a presence about him." And it held true throughout our time in Fiji, even though we worked under James for only a short time. He remained our steadfast and very close friend.

The first time I saw James standing on the wharf at Suva, he was dressed in jungle shorts and shirt with sandals on his feet, his large girth quite obvious, and a happy face with a dark close-cropped beard.

"Bula!" said James as we were introduced to him. In typical Fijian fashion, James grasped our hands in the loose limpid grip of a Fijian handshake.

We proceeded to make small talk and James said, "I usually travel by boat whenever I come down to Suva." Charlie asked, "Why is that James?" And James smiled while replying, "Well, I don't really like to fly and anyway the seats in the airplane are pretty small for me!" We all had a good laugh at that. We were hitting it off very well with our new friend, Big James Makasiale.

My journal entry for February 5 notes:

"...finally left Suva at 7:00 p.m. on the Fijian Princess. The weather is clear and sea fairly calm for my first ride on the ocean. I did start to get seasick, like being dizzy, and with stomach upset. But I made it through the whole trip without heaving up once. I slept on the deck where it was fairly cool and comfortable. After an all-night journey we arrived at Savusavu about 8:30 a.m. on February 6, 1968."

I recall that during that very first ocean voyage for this kid from Iowa, seasickness was a touch and go affair. Our friend, Big James, came to the aid that first night with a cure for my distressed condition.

As I lay on the open deck of the boat, trying without much luck to sleep, James came to see me. "How are you doing John?" he asked. I answered rather weakly, "Not very well. I think I'm getting sick."

James produced an orange and tearing off a piece of the peel said, "Here, squeeze and crush this and sniff it. It will help ease your seasickness." Gratefully I accepted the peel and did as he said. James left and I began sniffing that peel for all it was worth. Surprisingly, my condition improved. The orange peel seasickness cure worked.

When I got the slightest inclination to be sick during that voyage, I would simply sniff the orange peel and my symptoms would disappear.

James returned later and inquired, "John, how are you doing now? You OK?" With a weak smile I answered, "Hey James, thanks for the orange peel. This stuff really helps." James nodded approvingly and walked away. I have always been grateful to my friend, Big James, for making my very first ocean voyage a more tolerable experience.

And so, we sailed off on the Fijian Princess into the moonlit and star bright Fijian night. We crossed the Pacific waters and as dawn broke, we awoke and entered what looked like another world entirely.

But we knew that this must be the place. This was Vanua Levu, Savusavu Bay, the coastline of Cakaudrove Province. Stretching up the coast were coconut trees which seemed to go on and on in an infinite line, like soldiers guarding tbe beaches. It was an ethereal world, a somehow unreal view, a scene that should be just a figment of our imagination. The early dawn rays of sun glistening on the coconut trees lent a fairyland aura to the whole scene. But this was real. This was going to be our place for the next couple of years.

After all the trials and frustrations, all the ambiguities and uncertainties, our time had come. We were about to step into another world altogether. It was a world from which we would return as different individuals. Our personal life adventures had just been kicked up a notch.

CHAPTER 3

ON VANUA LEVU

As the Fijian Princess slipped through the reef and safely entered Savusavu Bay, we stood transfixed and enthralled by the view unfolding before us. The early morning sun accented the coastal areas of the island. It highlighted the magnificent coconut groves, the beaches, the surf breaking over the reef, and contrasted sharply with the dark gray clouds hanging over the surrounding green hills and blue lagoons of the bay.

Vanua Levu is a volcanic high island as opposed to a low-lying coral atoll. It does share similarities however, such as a surrounding coral reef, enclosed lagoons, and groves of the ever-present coconut palm.

However, the stark contrast comes when one views the foreboding hills and interior peaks, some towering to over 3000 ft. elevation and covered with dense tropical rain forest.

Vanua Levu, being the second largest island of Fiji, has an area of some 2,137 square miles, about half the size of Viti Levu, the main island. The province of Cakaudrove encompasses the southern and eastern coasts and peninsula of the island. The provincial center is Savusavu.

The province also includes the islands of Taveuni, Kioa, Rabi, and assorted other smaller islands to the east. Cakaudrove is on the windward wet side of the island, thus its heavy stands of jungle, rain forest, and coconut groves. The southern and western areas of Vanua Levu tend to be dryer and thus account for the sugar cane grown in Macuata and Bua Provinces.

As we approached the wharf in Savusavu Bay, we knew that this was Vanua Levu and not Suva. And it certainly was not Honolulu or San Francisco or anywhere near the USA. As the dawn broke open into bright daylight, so did it dawn on us that we had finally arrived at our island.

"Wow, would you believe this view?" Dave shouted in excitement, "It looks like something straight out of James Michener."

"Man, this is really a far-out place!" added Charlie, taking in the scene. "Just look at those coconut trees. There must be millions of them," he exclaimed.

"Yeah Charlie, and don't forget, you're going to have to count every damned one of those trees too for this census work we're going to do," I said emphatically.

Paul chimed in and said, "Well, I think we're just going to have to estimate those bloody things. We'd be here forever counting them one at a time!"

"Yeah, but just keep in mind you guys, they may be sending us out here to stay forever. Maybe nobody will even remember we came here," I added facetiously.

Big James came strolling up to join us at the bow of the boat as she headed into port. "Well you guys, this is it. This is Vanua Levu. What do you think so far?" he asked.

"Oh James, it's fantastic. It's beautiful," said Dave. Charlie added, "Is the entire province like this, as picturesque and lovely?"

"Well," said James casually, "you guys will get your chance to find that out soon enough."

"How soon will be going out into the countryside James?" Paul asked.

"Well, we'll get out there and show you guys around just as soon as we are rested up from this trip. Remember, you are going to be here for two years. You'll have plenty of time to see the sights," James replied.

"James, I just can't get over this. The scenery is incredible. This is all just like a dream," I said.

James countered seriously, "You guys will find out soon enough the difference between dreaming and reality. Vanua Levu is no dream. Behind that dreamy beautiful exterior lies a land of harsh reality. A reality of a hard way of life for most of the people who live here. That is what you've come here to learn about and maybe even do something about, right? So, let's get going."

As the boat pulled up to the wharf, we got our first close look at the town of Savusavu. The town, an outpost really, had a population of about 2000 then. It hugs the eastern shoreline of Savusavu Bay, surrounded by green hills, the blue lagoon of the bay, and coconuts that seem to stretch forever along the coastline.

The town had one road which winds along the coastline. Along the road on either side are a hodgepodge of small shops and buildings housing general stores, trading companies, barber shops, tailors, and sundry others generally run by ambitious Indian and Chinese merchants. The smaller shops are usually wood frame, iron-roofed structures so typical of the South Pacific islands.

At the southern end of town, near the wharf, is the venerable old Planters' Club, that supposedly aristocratic elite establishment open exclusively to the coconut planters' society of Cakaudrove Province. The coconut planters were the mostly European plantation owners who were large landholders and owned most of the larger commercial copra plantations of the province. The Planters' Club was a holdout of the once proud and powerful colonial era aristocracy. It was also one of the few places in town where one could buy cold beer. Generally, one needed to know someone who belonged to the club to gain entry.

Continuing up the road into town were the Burns Philip Ltd. and Morris-Hedstrom general stores, two of the South Pacific's well-known trading companies. These two traders handled much of the copra trade and supplied the island with many of the everyday wares and goods.

These two stores were the focal point of the town, such as it was at that time, in 1968. Another center of interest at that time was the Hot Springs Hotel, located above and behind the two general stores. The Hot Springs, so named for the bubbling thermal stream located on the hotel grounds, was a rambling old wooden structure with airy rooms and lobby, bar, and wide verandas. It was a real South Pacific landmark in Savusavu. The hotel sat on a hill a block back from the road and bay. It provided a magnificent view of Savusavu Bay and the western hills of Vanua Levu, stretching to the southwest.

The hotel bar and veranda became a gathering place of sorts for us during those early days. We would go there to relax in the quaint pleasant surroundings and to drink a few bottles of delicious icy cold Fiji Beer. To our dismay however, we soon learned that the hotel's days were numbered. It had been sold to the Travelodge hotel chain and they planned to demolish the old structure and build a new one. So it was that the hotel closed in the middle of our first year in Cakaudrove, leaving us temporarily without a bar in which to drink. But that is another story.

On up the road, somewhat away from the business area of town was a separate government compound. Here were located the police station, courthouse, agriculture office, post office, telephone exchange and the district officer's headquarters.

As the road continued and wound away from the shoreline of Savusavu Bay, it passed through Yaroi Village, a settlement of several hundred Fijians. From here, the road moved inland, leaving the bay, passing the government housing compound, and on to Savusavu

Hospital. The road branches off near the hospital and runs out to Savurekareka Catholic Mission on the other side of Savusavu Bay. The road also turns in the opposite direction and goes out into the bush area north of Savusavu to Savudrodro Village and a government farming area. Out in this area, two miles past the hospital was the small settlement of Tavutikau, where Dave Reed's bure was located.

A journal entry from February 1968, describes Savusavu:

"...Savusavu is merely a small settlement strung out around the bay here, though there are several shops and stores and even a movie house just about completed! We are staying at our AO's (agriculture officer) house here, James Makasiale. I'll be with him for about one month until my bure is finished up in Tukavesi, my village. Vanua Levu is really beautiful. It is so hilly, and the bays and coral shores are many. Coconut trees are everywhere...looks like we'll have plenty of work. I thought there was more to Fiji than just Suva!"

Altogether, the town stretched along a good five miles from boat wharf to the hospital. And most of the town was located directly on the lone road fronting the bay. Many of the people lived in huts or houses on or near the road or up in the hills that rose up from the narrow coastal flatland.

The biggest problem with the town's layout was the obvious distance between points. It was not a convenient town at all. Nothing was centrally located. As we were soon to learn, everything was a good walking distance away, regardless of where you were in the town. But we soon got used to all of that. In fact, we soon got used to the idea of walking anywhere, no matter how great the distance. In the bush of Cakaudrove, walking was often the only mode of transportation.

Upon arrival in Savusavu that first morning, we were met by an agriculture department Land Rover. This was our first meeting with the department driver, Ram Nand, who was to become a good friend. Ram was Indian and had an infectious laugh, ready smile, and a friendly nature. He, like many of the Indians in Fiji, was multi-lingual. He spoke Hindi, Fijian, and English. English was of course the official language of then colonial Fiji.

We collected our gear from the Fijian Princess and loaded it into the waiting Land Rover. We then drove up the lone road that was Savusavu and had our first close up look at the town. It was a real eye opener, straight out of an old fashioned South Pacific yarn. The road coursed along the narrow coastal flatland fronting the bay. The foothills to the island's interior peaks began their rise almost from the water's edge, at least in some places. The colorful shops, stores, and houses hugged the road, some on water's edge and some on the slopes immediately behind the road. Where there were not coconut trees there was a heavy stand of dense jungle or heavy reed grass (which we called elephant grass). The shoreline was often clogged with dense stands of mangrove trees.

"Well you guys," James said (he always called us "you guys" in an obvious attempt to be American), "this is Savusavu. It's a long way from Suva."

"Wow, I'll say it is," Dave replied. "There sure aren't many buildings around here," noted Charlie.

"Yeah, and the ones that are here have got to be ancient already," added Paul. "Man, this is really a desolate looking place. Is it really a town James?" I asked curiously.

"Well, it's not really much of a town you guys. It is more like a settlement. It dates from long ago and it hasn't changed much in recent years," James explained.

"Wow, the buildings are sure something. The whole place looks like it stepped right out of a book," Dave said.

James warned, "You guys better get used to it. This is going to be the biggest town you'll ever see up here in Cakaudrove. The only place bigger is Labasa, and that's up over the mountains on the west side of the island."

We drove through the town to the government housing compound. Here the town's civil servants lived in comfortable western style housing. We arrived at James's house and were met by his beautiful wife, Nuku, an outgoing and friendly Lauan woman. Like James, she was also of fair complexion and appeared more Polynesian than Melanesian.

We unloaded our gear and got settled into the comfortable surroundings and environment of James and Nuku Makasiale's home. Nuku had rooms ready for us so we paired off and shared rooms. But the atmosphere was certainly not the barracks or dormitory style living which had been our usual accommodations the past several weeks. James and Nuku had plenty of room in the large home as they had no children of their own.

This fact was to play an important role in establishing our relationship over the next several days and weeks with both James and Nuku. For it was to turn out that Nuku, or "Aunt Nuku," as we would fondly call her, adopted us as her own.

For the present, Nuku, knowing how exhausted we would be after the all-night boat ride from Suva, had a nice breakfast ready in a short time. We had eggs, bacon, and some of the best scones any of us had ever had. It was only one of many wonderful and satisfying meals that Aunt Nuku would prepare for us.

After our breakfast, we collapsed in our rooms for the rest of the day. The four of us were content for the time being. We had a comfortable place to stay and we had made it at long last to our destination, the island of Vanua Levu. It would not be long until we were out exploring our new home. Tomorrow we would begin our new job responsibilities.

The next day, Wednesday, February 7, 1968, dawned clear and bright, foretelling a typical warm summer Fijian day. Down under the equator where Fiji lies, the seasons are just the opposite from the northern hemisphere. February is considered the latter part of summer.

This was our second day in Savusavu, and we were eager to get going and check out the area. Together with James, we rode down to the provincial agriculture office which was to be our working headquarters. Being prim and proper in British colonial Fiji, one always referred to the main office as "headquarters." This stemmed from the straight laced, staunch, and very militaristic approach the colonial British took toward all their affairs. It was the type of attitude that typified the British in Fiji, and one to which we as unattached, young, and somewhat anti-establishment Americans often poked fun at and even mocked by humorous attempts at imitating the British. We never acted aloof toward our friends, the local people. To them, we were always just those young Americans who came to live and work among them. This was the foundation of our relationship which carried us through the difficult months ahead.

We arrived at the office and were introduced to all the agriculture staff. Here again the strong colonial militaristic tradition was much in evidence. Most of the staff members were one type of "officer" or another. Under the agriculture officer, who was responsible for the entire province's agriculture development, was a staff hierarchy composed of a livestock officer, a forestry officer, a finance officer, and several field officers who in turn had a variety of field assistants, clerks, and typists under them. The arrangement was strictly adhered to in the communication process. Here one learned to follow channels and quickly got familiar with the pecking order.

At any rate, the staff were all friendly and outgoing and seemed pleased to have us aboard. They went out of their way to show us genuine welcome to the province. Most of the staff were Fijian, except for Ram, the driver, and the finance officer who controlled disbursement of funds, both Indian. There were also a couple of part-Europeans on the staff and one or two others of various ethnic groups.

After introductions all around, we got down to organizing our work which was to be supervision of the very first agriculture census for Cakaudrove Province. Cakaudrove covered a large area including the entire southeastern portion of Vanua Levu plus the islands of Taveuni, Kioa, Rabi, Laucala, Gamea, and the atolls of Yacata, Yunuca and Nggelelevu. This was an area that covered hundreds of square miles of water and land, an area that had few roads, unreliable transportation, and at best, a fair communication system. It was for all practical purposes, one of the least developed provinces of Fiji.

We began our work by sorting out the aerial photographs with which each of us would be working. Since we volunteers would oversee direct supervision of the census in our respective areas of the province, we needed to familiarize ourselves with the terrain via the photographs.

We also needed to get an overview of the project as we would be supervising one or two local enumerators who would be assisting us in the actual field work of surveying a farmer's land and counting his crops and animals. Our enumerators would be coming in soon for a first meeting with us and we wanted to look organized and prepared for the work. This even though in the early planning stage we often wondering just how to go about all this.

The journal entry for February 7, 1968, notes:

"...began work today here in Savusavu. Sorted out the aerial photos for each area. What a job since we changed the original areas around some. Put in quite a day. Did get into the country for a while this morning. Still amazed at the beauty of this land. This evening we came home and partook of several bowls of yaqona. These sessions usually last for a couple of hours or more before supper is taken. I can say that one is darned hungry by the time he eats. I am getting used to drinking yaqona though. It's not bad stuff."

(Note: yaqona is Fiji's national drink, the pounded root of the piper methysticum plant; also known as kava throughout the South Pacific and commonly called grog in Fiji, it's the basis of much socializing; the pounded root is mixed with water in a large wooden basin and looks like dirty muddy water; while it's non-alcoholic it generally has a soporific numbing and relaxing effect, making one lethargic and sleepy.)

It was soon after this that we had our first meeting with our enumerators. These men, all young strong Fijians from the various areas of Cakaudrove would be doing the bulk of the actual field enumeration work. The province was divided roughly into the equivalent of counties and each enumerator would be working in one or two county areas. We went over the division of work responsibilities, the areas each man would be responsible for and decided to have frequent census team meetings to monitor the progress.

We as the supervisors were to play a dual role, that of overseeing the work of our co-workers and to do some of the actual field enumeration work ourselves. Over and above these we also played another, though less obvious role, of American living in a Fijian village. This would be the step that would soon carry us out into the bush and would be the reason behind our eventual immersion into the Fijian culture. To each of us individually, this was perhaps the most important role. For in this role, in our individual relationships with the people, we learned about each other. That is what the Peace Corps is all about.

The first several days in Savusavu were spent organizing our work. We also took some trips out into the countryside to familiarize ourselves with the area. James was a great leader in that he tried so hard to make things easy for us. By taking us on familiarization tours through the area and opening his own home to us with generous hospitality, he was helping us make the transition from our past to the realities of everyday living in Fiji. He knew the difficulties of adjustment we faced because he himself had been through similar experiences when he first went to Hawai`i to study.

One of the first trips we took, apart from the general vicinity of Savusavu, was up to Buca Bay, the area in which I would be working. Buca Bay, which means "flat bay" in Fijian, was located on the south-eastern peninsula of Cakaudrove Province. Buca Bay lies on the eastern face of this peninsula with the islands of Kioa and Rabi across the bay and the island of Taveuni across the straits of the ocean beyond.

The first village we visited was Tukavesi, the government center for Buca Bay. This is where I would eventually be located when my bure, a bamboo thatched grass roofed hut, was built. Because of funding delays and even indecision on the part of the Peace Corps and the agriculture department as to where we would be posted, my housing was late in getting built. Tukavesi was a village of some 300 people but the various government facilities made it seem larger. People from the surrounding area came to Tukavesi to obtain the various government services including medical treatment. Located here were the agriculture station, the medical clinic, the government primary (elementary) school and the public works department which maintained the road.

It should be noted that Buca Bay lies some forty miles east of Savusavu on an excellent gravel road, the Hibiscus Highway. This is one of the best roads, the only road really, in Cakaudrove Province. And thanks to the men of the PWD, the road crew, the highway was always in excellent condition, at least in most places and in the worst of weather conditions.

At the Buca Bay agriculture station, I met the field officer with whom I would be working and living, Savenaca Koroinivalu, his wife, Marama, and their five children. I met them only briefly but eventually would come to know and love this family very much. I was later to become an integral part of their family.

From Tukavesi we toured the rest of the Buca Bay area and stopped at Nawi, a remote village near the end of the road on the southeast side of the bay. This was the village of my co-worker for the census, Josefa Nayavadrega. We stopped here for part of the afternoon, engaged in some "vosa vaka Viti," (Fiji talk), and drank several rounds of yaqona. It was quite an experience and still stands out in my mind. We were sitting in a remote Fijian village in the chief's house, trying to converse in an unfamiliar language and trying to get used to the customs of the place.

The second week of our stay in Savusavu began with another familiarization trip. This time we headed for Charlie Matthews' post at Korotasere up on Natewa Bay. We traveled up and over the hill from Savusavu, down past the airport, and followed the beautiful Hibiscus Highway through the plantations of coconut palms that covered the coastal areas of Cakaudrove.

The highway passed directly through many coconut groves and meandered up the coastline, twisting and turning as it went. The road passed by sparkling coral beaches, beautiful coral reefs, quiet bays and magnificent coconut groves, and some dank mangrove swamps as well.

Midway up to Buca Bay, the road branches to the north and heads to Natewa Bay. The bay lies at a northeast to southwest angle, to the southeast lies the Buca Bay peninsula and to the northwest, the main bulk of Vanua Levu.

As it turned out, Charlie had the most inaccessible post of us all. Korotasere was reached only by boat or by walking up the coast. From the end of the road at the lower end of the bay it was some twenty miles. Charlie was definitely in the bush.

But for all of us it was a real thrill and delight to be seeing all this countryside. We were fortunate to have the opportunity to travel around and see so much and this would prove to be a real asset later on in our service.

My journal entry for February 12, 1968, notes:

"…took a trip up Natewa Bay to take Charlie Matthews to Korotasere and his assignment. Nice boat ride and beautiful country. Charlie has a beautiful bure in a nice location. We were up until 3:30 a.m. The people just don't know when to leave. It's going to be hard to get used to these ceremonies and customs in the villages here."

We were getting a quick introduction to the Fijian love for fun. It seemed that no matter where we went, the yaqona bowl came out, the guitars warmed up, and the village girls began asking us to dance. For the Fijians, in their often-remote isolated villages, it was a big event to have foreign visitors and Americans on top of that. It was good enough reason to have a party. It was a scene that would be repeated many times in our visits to the bush villages of Cakaudrove over the next several months.

We stayed overnight, or what was left of it anyway, in Charlie's bure and returned to Savusavu the next day. We said our farewells to Charlie and left him on his own to live in Korotasere. It was the beginning of a truly satisfying and happy life for Charlie. Even though he was in a remote area he would thrive on the activity he planned for himself. Perhaps more than any of the rest of us, Charlie got deeply involved in the Fijian culture. This was due in part to his own skill and ambition and partly to the close relationship, trust, and confidence that he developed with the people of Korotasere and the Vaturova district of Cakaudrove.

No sooner had we returned to Savusavu on Tuesday, February 13, than we were off onto yet another trip. We headed back up the Hibiscus Highway on the February 14, to Buca Bay to catch the boat to Taveuni.

We were to deliver Paul Korenberg to his assignment on the north end of Taveuni at the Bouma agriculture station.

Getting to Taveuni from Buca Bay was a challenge. At Nutuvu, Buca Bay, a couple of Indians operated a dilapidated old launch that served as a shuttle boat of sorts across Buca Bay and the Somosomo Straits to Taveuni. On a calm clear day, the boat ride takes about three or four hours to cross a distance of six to eight miles.

The launch leaves the Nutuvu landing in the early morning and reaches the Waiyevo, Taveuni, landing just before midday. The first leg of the boat ride is uneventful. The boat crosses Buca Bay's calm serene waters protected from the open ocean by Kioa Island setting directly in the middle of the bay. From Nutuvu, the boat goes directly east, passing the villages of Vunikura and Nawi on the southern shore of Buca Bay and then past Kioa. From here the boat enters more open and exposed waters coming from the north. The coastline of lower Buca Bay drops away sharply to the southeast. As the boat goes further, it enters into the Somosomo Straits, which is an expanse of some two or three miles where the ocean can send its swells and currents passing between Kioa, the Buca Bay peninsula, and the island of Taveuni.

During my two years there, I crossed the straits many times and can say, fortunately, that I never encountered any grave danger. However, the passage was potentially dangerous. If the weather was bad, the swells and currents could be especially tricky for a small foundering boat, such as the Buca Bay launch.

At the time not much concern was expressed over this matter. The launch was as safe and dependable as any of the old launches running the passage. Besides, it was the only one operating with any kind of regular schedule and it was cheap. The charge was only fifty cents for the one-way ride. The boat would go over in the morning and return in the afternoon, usually. It made the trip about three times weekly. There was one time, later during my service, when I spent a couple of days sitting at the Waiyevo agriculture office waiting for that boat. Because of the situation at the time, there was literally nothing for me to do but sit and wait. My work was finished but there was nothing I could do except be patient and wait.

The journal for Wednesday, May 22, 1968, notes:

"...guess I'll be here till Friday since there is no passenger boat for tomorrow. So will just spend another day here whiling away the time..."

The journal continues Friday, May 24, 1968:

"...so here I am sitting at the Waiyevo landing. It's still early morning and the boat doesn't come till noon or after. Guess I'll just kill some more time. I hope to catch the Land Rover at Nutuvu this afternoon and then on to Savusavu again."

The boat did come, and I did make it safely, once again, over the water from Taveuni to Vanua Levu.

The island of Taveuni is a special place in Fijian culture and history. It is a chiefly island and the village of Somosomo was the home of the paramount chief, Tui Cakau, or King of the Reef. By Fijian tradition, Tui Cakau is powerful as is the province of Cakaudrove. It was the one province that was not conquered by Cakobau, the King of Fiji, in the early 1800's when it was common for Fiji's tribes to carry on civil war.

Taveuni is shaped somewhat like a loaf of French bread, a rather elongated island with a flat oval shape. It is a beautiful island, stretching long and magnificent into the ocean like an ancient warrior canoe. By day it is crowned with a long white cloud. The island rises directly from the ocean and slopes gradually to a fairly high elevation. The narrow coastal flats and the slopes of the island are dense with coconut trees. The fertile soil and dense rain forest merited Taveuni the local name, "The Garden Island."

Geographically, the island lies in a northeastern to southwestern direction. It is bisected almost in the midsection by the 180th. Meridian, the International Dateline.

There are many privately owned coconut plantations on the island. Many of these represent the elite aristocracy of the rigid colonial system. Many of these plantations have existed for many years, owned, and handed down from generation to generation of the European families that operate them.

The journal for February 14, 1968, notes:

"...traveled to the island of Taveuni today. Took Paul to his bure in Bouma, but he can't move in yet as there is some difficulty over payment for construction by the agriculture department. Taveuni is a beautiful place, nice sand beaches around in many places."

The problem of Paul's housing, or lack of it, was probably a factor in his ultimate decision to transfer down to Viti Levu, which he did in a short time. There was a dispute between the villagers of Bouma who built his bure on contract with the agriculture department. They apparently had not been paid and did not want the house occupied until they were paid. They even threatened to "kama na vale," burn the house down if they weren't paid.

So, Paul had to locate back down at the Waiyevo government housing area. Psychologically, this was not a pleasant experience and no doubt left strained feelings on both sides, with Paul in the middle. Being new volunteers also, we did not fully understand the situation.

The February 15, 1968, journal entry notes:

"...left Paul in Waiyevo at government housing. Don't know what will happen yet regarding his permanent housing. He's practically in the same boat as me...without a home!"

Dave's housing situation was secure on the other hand. He was assigned to a Fijian style bure in Tavutikau, a small settlement near the village of Savudrodro, a couple of miles outside of Savusavu town. His bure was located below the house of the Roko Tui, a chief of the provincial government. He shared the compound with some other provincial government workers and their families.

With Dave situated in his own bure outside of Savusavu, I was now the only one left who was not out on his assignment. It was again a period of transition. I had a job to do but no place from which to do it. It was a situation that would be somewhat frustrating over the next several weeks as I awaited my own bure to be built up at Buca Bay. Until then, I was somewhat "footloose and fancy free" as the saying goes, and I tried to make the best of it.

The February 15, 1968, journal entry notes:

"...am happy to have been able to see much of Vanua Levu and Taveuni. Really beautiful lands here in Fiji. Hope to get some good pictures later of the islands."

Little did I know then just what lay ahead of me.

CHAPTER 4

LEARNING TO LIVE FIJIAN STYLE

After the rigors of several familiarization tours throughout the province, it was nice to be able to relax for a change. James and Nuku, with whom I was still staying in Savusavu, took Dave and me on a beach picnic outing. This weekend, February 16-18, 1968, marked our first month in Fiji. Time was moving along.

However, time was beginning to hang heavily on my hands once again. The other fellows, Dave, Charlie, and Paul were out on the job, so to speak, but I was still stuck in Savusavu. I tried to be patient and to take things in stride.

To at least start getting my feet wet and begin learning about the job I was sent here to do, I was to leave on Monday, February 19, for Buca Bay. I was to spend a couple of days at the village of Nawi where my census co-worker, Josefa, lived.

This little field trip would accomplish two things. First, it would get me out of Savusavu and into the field, and second, it would put me into the village where I would start learning how to live Fijian style. I ended up spending my time between Nawi and Savusavu over the next several weeks while my housing situation was being decided.

I was driven up to Nawi by Land Rover, another jostling trip via the Hibiscus Highway. Before two years were up, I would become very familiar with the forty or so miles of road connecting Buca Bay with Savusavu.

At Nawi, I was housed with the Agriculture Department field man, Iskeli Tuiwainunu, or Tui, as we called him. He was a young fellow about my age, perhaps a year or two older. His boss was Savenaca, the Field Officer/Buca Bay, stationed at Tukavesi (my eventual location).

Tui welcomed me into his bure and helped me set up my bed and other gear. Along with Josefa, my co-worker, we got along very well, and both helped me considerably in those first few days of being in a village. Both had secondary schooling and could speak English quite well, so this was a great help to me. They helped me greatly in learning Fijian also.

My journal entry for February 19th notes:

"...I went to village of Nawi today, met Josefa and walked around the area a little. This was the first time I've been on my own in a village. Boy! That language is difficult. The Cakaudrove dialect is quite different from what I learned, the Bauan dialect. Luckily, there are English speakers here, or I'd be lost. I'm staying until Wednesday, then will return next week and stay until I have permanent housing somewhere in the Buca Bay area. My first impressions: I kind of feel like a PCV out in the field on my own. Then again, it's scary! This will be my first night in a village on my own. Excuse this writing, it's being written by kerosene lamp and it's not very bright."

I spent the next couple of days in Nawi just gathering my first impressions generally on being in a Fijian village. Together with Tui and Joe, I explored some of the local countryside around Nawi. I walked over to the village of Vunikura, three or four miles up the coast from Nawi.

I was fortunate to have Tui as a friend, as well as Joe. I learned a lot from them both: customs, language, how to get around in the village and they provided answers to my many questions. The language was difficult but necessary to learn for survival. I did my best to practice and improve on what skill I had.

I was expecting to be in Nawi for only a short time until my bure (house) was completed over at Tukavesi on the other side of Buca Bay. So, for now, Nawi was all right. It provided me an introduction to village living and the field work I would be doing on the census.

Tui told me that I would be better off in Tukavesi where there was a medical dispensary, the agriculture station, stores, and a good water supply. In comparison, Nawi had few services available, other than a small village store that sold tobacco, kerosene, sugar, soap, and tea. Furthermore, Nawi was located far down the road, away from the Buca Bay center. The road had a very steep winding hill that led down to Nawi. It was not travelled by the Buca Bay "jungle bus" as the bus could not negotiate the hill. So, in fact, Nawi was isolated despite being located on the road. The road had little vehicle traffic.

During the next few weeks, I would have the invigorating experience of rising at dawn to hike up that hill, follow the road to Vunikura and on to Nutuvu landing where the bus stopped. This was the only way to catch the early morning bus, the only bus, going to Savusavu. On occasion, I was able to ask the local Indian taxi driver to pick me up at Nawi. But often, I had to walk the five or six miles over to catch the bus.

I remember well that walk to Nutuvu. My alarm clock awoke me very early, even before most of Nawi was awake. The sun was just turning the sky pink on the eastern horizon, behind Taveuni Island. Since no one else was awake and I had no cooking facilities in the bure where I slept, I left without any breakfast. I would dress, pulling on shirt, shorts, and jungle boots. I would then pack other gear in my backpack and be off.

Nawi sets on a flat coastal strip surrounded by coconut groves. At the back of the village, the road passes by and starts rising sharply to the west. The hill is a long steep grade, covered only with loose gravel that makes the walk difficult. It is hard to get sure footing.

The Nawi hill is the most difficult part of the entire walk over to Nutuvu. It is about a mile or more long, winding up through the hills and forest. The road rises from sea level to probably 1200-ft. elevation at the summit of the hill. Once at the summit, I was drenched with perspiration even through it was still early morning and the sun low in the sky. The humidity was high and that made the walk hard.

Winding down the western slope was much easier of course. The sun was blocked, providing cool shade that was a welcome relief and made the walk down a breeze. At the bottom of the slope was a relatively flat stretch of road leading into Vunikura village and onto the seacoast again. It then followed the coast onto the Nutuvu landing where the bus stop was.

It was a pleasant early morning walk. It was a time to take in the beautiful pristine countryside of the real Fiji. It was a time to try to sort out my thoughts. If for no other reason, the walk was necessary because it was the only way for me to get out of Nawi, unless I wanted to wait indefinitely for the Agriculture Department Land Rover. One thing that kept me going was the prospect of a big breakfast in Savusavu when I got there. Eggs, meat, bread, coffee, these were things worth walking up the Nawi hill for at such an early morning hour.

In addition to the general culture shock one experiences upon being thrust into a foreign culture, one also must adjust to a myriad of changes. Language, terrain, housing, sanitary facilities, and food were just a few adjustments that the Peace Corps Volunteer in Fiji encountered.

Perhaps because it is one of the basics for survival, food was a critical adjustment for us. The average Fijian village diet is heavy on starch and carbohydrates and short on protein. Starch foods such as rice and root crops of dalo, cassava, and yams predominate. Breadfruit is also a seasonal food used widely and perhaps even preferable to the other starch foods.

In many areas of Fiji, fish is a staple, especially fresh fish from the ocean. Often however, fish in the diet (at least where I lived) was usually canned mackerel. Fresh meat was scarce and meat in the diet was often in the form of canned corned beef. In Buca Bay, the villagers did little fishing, except on special occasions. At times there would be small shallow water fish available, often caught by the women with nets.

The initial adjustment to a tea, cassava, dalo, yam, rice, and fish diet was a hard one. First, the food was simply hard to eat. To the uninitiated palate, it was dry, starchy, bland, and completely tasteless. At first, a mouthful was chewed and chewed and gradually swallowed, but it required a supreme effort. Lots of tea helped to wash it down.

During the first few weeks in the village, I often finished a meal totally unsatisfied. Hunger returned shortly after eating. What was consumed did not stay long. It was a matter of developing a taste for the fare being offered. We ate but often forced ourselves to eat.

Visions of hamburgers, pizza, eggs, milk, and hundreds of other things played on our imagination. There was no cupboard or refrigerator to raid at night. No readily available snacks were to be had. It was a completely humbling experience. Only after several weeks' adjustment did we begin to get comfortable with the diet.

I think we never fully adjusted to the diet. Perhaps it was a case of tolerating it only. I recall that later as I made frequent trips into Savusavu, one of my biggest pleasures was the anticipation of a good meal or two at one of the cafes in town. There we could get fresh beef and mutton (goat) along with eggs, bread, etc. This was a welcome change of fare from the village diet.

Our favorite rendezvous in Savusavu became Ping Ho's Café or Vale ni Kana (House of Food). Ping's was located directly on the road in Savusavu about midway in the settlement. It was an antiquated wooden building with metal roof, the usual type of structure, and painted a bright blue green. On the sign advertising Ping Ho's Café, it also stated seriously, "Delicious Chinese Dishes." The only problem with that was the fact that the only Chinese food Ping's ever had was beef chop suey. The rest of the menu covered the usual eggs, beef, pork, and mutton curry.

Ping Ho was in his late 60's and was from China. He had been in the islands quite a while. He had ended up here in Savusavu and had opened his café years ago. We became good friends with Ping and he always enjoyed having us stop in his café.

As was typical of the fine relationship we enjoyed with most of the people of Cakaudrove, we got along well with Ping. He often fixed us special meals, or added a special little dessert, whenever we turned up at his café, tired and hungry. Ping Ho's was a Peace Corps hangout in Savusavu.

Comparable to the adjustment we made to the diet was the adjustment we made to drinking Fiji's national drink, yaqona or kava, or as it is called in Fiji, grog. Made from the pounded root and pulp of the piper methysticum plant, a member of the pepper family, yaqona was essentially soporific rather than intoxicating. It is non-alcoholic. It brought on drowsiness, lethargy, and loss of appetite when consumed in large quantities, which it usually was.

Used throughout much of the South Pacific islands as a ceremonial drink, in Fiji it was ceremonial as well as traditional and common. It was the national pastime to drink grog. There is not a village in Fiji where grog is not drunk. A grog session provides a general socializing for villagers to talk story, exchange news, views, and play games, notably caroms, checkers, and cards.

A grog session is Fiji's version of a beer bust. It can include the whole village or just a few people. It can serve as focus for a dance or as a fund-raising event for the village church, school, or club.

Grog has the appearance of muddy water. It is brownish gray in color depending upon the yaqona plant used and whether it is dried or green. The pounded root powder or pulp is mixed in a large carved basin called a "tanoa" and served in a half coconut shell called a "bilo." The taste is almost indescribable but leaves a numbing sensation on the tongue and lips, tasting like floured water with slightly gritty peppery flavor and texture.

Grog is a diuretic, a stimulant to the kidneys. At first, when trying to get used to this and the change in diet, the whole urinary and excretory systems are affected.

After a time and so much practice, grog drinking became second nature to us. We even began to crave the stuff to an extent, even though it was non-addictive. To the people, the villagers with whom we lived, it was a supreme compliment that we enjoyed drinking grog with them. They were completely amazed at our ability to really get into yaqona drinking. Perhaps too, we amazed ourselves. There were times when we really enjoyed drinking the stuff, primarily because of the camaraderie it brought about with the Fijians.

Among the other changes which we had to make were bathing in streams and using an outhouse or the bushes to answer nature's calls. Bathing in a stream was not so bad if one could find some privacy and it had not been raining. Often it was necessary to wear swim shorts to bathe in because there would be people passing by the stream right when you were in the act. The shorts at least protected your decency which otherwise would be subject to the scrutiny of curious villagers.

I recall a particularly humbling experience in Nawi when bathing one afternoon with some of the village boys. I was not wearing shorts and they all stood around eagerly eyeballing the "kai vavalagi," (the foreigner) to see how he measured up. Simply, they wanted to see if Americans were any different.

Lots or rapid discussion and comments were exchanged among them as I stripped and plunged into the stream. I tried my best to be modest, but it was difficult to hide everything in a stream three feet wide and one foot deep. At least they found out that I was not all the same shade of white!

The outhouse plumbing was something else. Many of the latrines in the villages were water seal type. This was a cement slab with a hole (and if you were lucky a stool to sit on) and a U-shaped neck underneath. The water seal kept the odor level down and aided in controlling pests like flies. It was a real improvement over the old-fashioned outhouse with just a hole in the ground.

But even though the outhouses were halfway sanitary, for a westerner, it was still hard to get used to squatting, which is what one often had to do. The whole thing made a modern water tank toilet a most enjoyable luxury when we came across one in our travels. The worst thing about a Fijian outhouse made of simple coconut leaf thatch and bamboo was making a dash for one in the rain and finding it leaking, which it usually did. It was such an unpleasantry at a most necessary time.

In relation to housing, we found out early that complete privacy was not possible in a Fijian house. Custom dictated that a house is open to whomever wishes to enter. You never turn people away from your house. That would be very rude.

Also, any visitors who do stop in must be visited with. You are expected to drop what you are doing and talk with that person. It all added up to a lack of privacy for the Peace Corps Volunteer. This was a most difficult adjustment to make.

Frequently in those early days of my time in the villages, I had a burning desire to just be alone. This just was not possible. Someone was always with me no matter where I went or what I did. It was the people's way of making me feel welcome to make sure I would not get lonely. This was especially true at Nawi. Later, after I moved to Tukavesi, this became less of a problem. But at first it was a real strain, especially as I could not seem to be alone to gather my thoughts on my whole experience of just being there.

My housing in Nawi of course was shared with Tui. But we were both cared for, as far as meals go, by one of the families of Nawi. The family was headed by a man named Mariselo, and his wife, Pau. They were a middle-aged couple with about five or six children of their own plus assorted other relatives who shared their humble home.

I was taken in by this family, accepted without question, and well taken care of by them. They asked for nothing in return. Those very first few nights that I spent in Nawi are clear in my mind.

After the bath at the stream, Tui and I would sit in our bure talking until it was time to walk through the village to Mariselo and Pau's house for dinner. The evening meal usually consisted of fish and dalo, tavioka, or rice. Sometimes a cooked green leaf like spinach was included. Tea and hardtack crackers followed the meal.

Those first few weeks were very difficult for me. I liked the thrill and romance of being in a truly foreign setting and enjoyed the experiences of it all. There were times though when I felt very insecure and so helpless. The language of course was difficult for me but slowly I was learning it. The hardest part in those early days was not being adept enough in the language to carry on a good conversation or to directly answer questions. It helped a lot to have Tui and Josefa around. They would translate for me and act as my interpreter.

In those daily gatherings, either with the family group or with the villages in general, much of the conversation dealt with me. I often was the focal point of the people's curiosity, which was only natural. They wanted to know what I was doing there, where I came from, how long I would stay, and so on. It was a never-ending litany of question. Did I eat fish? Dalo? Tavioka? Did I drink yaqona? How well could I speak Fijian? How many people are there in America? What about Muhammad Ali? (Or was it Cassius Clay at that time?) And on and on.

These and a thousand other bits of trivia were the usual curiosities and questions brought up by the people. They were curious to the extent that their experiential background gave them a basis from which to expand their curiosity. What may have seemed trivial to us, however, was probably important to them. We often overlooked this point in considering their expanse of questions to us.

One very typical example of this is the Jim Reeves story. During our time in Fiji, 1968-69, Jim Reeves was undoubtedly the most popular western singer. His songs were heard frequently over Radio Fiji and his mellow rich voice and sad songs brought heart throbs to most Fijians. Jim Reeves was an American pop country singer who was killed in a plane crash in 1963.

The Fijians could not, would not, believe this fact. Everywhere we went during our two years, to the most isolated village of the island, somewhere, sometime, someone would inevitably ask the inevitable question, "Is Jim Reeves alive or dead?" And when the poor fellow was duly informed that good ole Jim was indeed dead, the second inevitable question followed, something like "Is he really dead?"

My friend Dave had a most amusing time with this story once in one of the villages he worked in. During a grog session the Jim Reeves story came up along with the inevitable questions about good ole Jim. By this time, Dave had become a rather good fabricator and added a new twist to an old story.

Dave, knowing the Fijians are very sentimental people, told the story that Jim Reeves had indeed died in a plane crash. But Jim had died,

Dave explained, because he had been jilted by a lover and, depressed and brokenhearted, had flown his airplane into a mountainside.

The Fijians ate it up! Because Jim Reeves sang such teary, heartsick, and melancholy songs, it just had to be true. Jim Reeves had killed himself because his lover had turned away from him.

One other story demonstrates how strong the belief was that Jim Reeves was not dead. Again, Dave is the key person in this story. Another village, another Fijian, asking Dave about the truth of Jim Reeves. Dave once again told the truth, but the man just could not accept it. "But David," he said, "we hear Jim Reeves on the radio every night. How can he be dead?"

Legends die hard, especially in Fiji.

One other notable worth mentioning is James Bond. Good ol' Secret Agent 007 was extremely popular during this time in Fiji. Many Fijians had heard of 007's exploits but few had actually seen the films of the '60s about James Bond. Nevertheless, 007 was as popular and as well known in the hinterlands of Cakaudrove Province as he was in Suva, the big city.

As Dave wrote home to his family in Maryland on November 5, 1968:

"...by the way, Fiji's greatest hero is none other than 007 himself. Fijian farmers paint 007 on their copra dryers. Indian stores sell James Bond shirts."

On Monday, March 4, 1968, I left Savusavu and the comforts of the temporary Peace Corps Hotel, better known as James and Nuku Makasiale's home. I was on my way back to Buca Bay and the village of Nawi. I had so far spent only a few days in the village and out in the field and was now going to start expanding my horizons again.

My journal entry for this day notes:

"...Nawi...guess I'll be here until they get my house built in Tukavesi. At the moment I'm somewhat pessimistic about the whole thing.

Staying here at Nawi won't be too bad though. It seems rather nice right now anyway. I hope to be here for only a couple of weeks, but I doubt if it will be that short of a time—considering Fijian time!"

Little did I then know just how long it would take me to get to Tukavesi and my own house. My patience would at times be stretched thin during this unsettling time.

And even though it was possibly a somewhat unsettling time for a new volunteer, it was in a way also settling. I became familiar with the people, the language, the culture, the countryside and how to survive in it. In short, I learned how to live Fijian style. Most of all, I started learning about myself and what I was capable of doing.

CHAPTER 5

THE AGRICULTURE CENSUS

The next several weeks went by rapidly and were quite eventful. I spent the two-month mark of being in Fiji out working in the field at the village of Vunikura just up the coast from Nawi. I had been waiting for some time to be out in the field, in the villages, getting to know the country, the work and the people.

Fortunately for me, I worked with Josefa from Nawi. Since he lived in the area and either knew or was related to many of the nearby villagers it was easy to work in the immediate area. I spent these first few weeks working in the villages of Nawi, Vunikura, Loa and Dakuniba.

I found out just what it was like to live and work in a very isolated rural area of Fiji. Even though there was a gravel road connecting these villages and leading to the Hibiscus Highway to Savusavu, the area was still very much isolated. The road carried at best, infrequent vehicle traffic. This was usually in the form of the PWD (Public Works Department) road crews who kept the weeds trimmed and roadway clear.

The local bus service extended only as far as Nutuvu landing, some five miles or so northwest of Nawi. So, there was little traffic to speak of on the lower end of this road passing through Vunikura, Nawi and to the end of the road at Dakuniba.

The road touched the coast at various points but basically travelled through the hills and valleys of the interior, winding through heavy jungle and rain forest and crossing numerous streams.

Most of the traffic amounted to the villagers walking from one village to another or the farmers walking from the village to their blocks of land where their farms were located. This of course was the major reason why the road had been built, to open the interior of the island to new block development. The village farmers could pioneer, or homestead a given block of land, usually about 30 acres or so, and would either live on the block or walk from the village. Thus, even though the road carried little motor traffic, it did serve the purpose of providing somewhat easier access to otherwise quite inaccessible lands.

Even with the road there, it was still a major effort to get out and walk for several miles to a farmer's block of land. Once there, the developing block had to be measured and the crops enumerated for the purposes of the agriculture census we were doing. It was difficult work to walk through the cleared land, avoiding rocks, tree roots, stumps, logs, struggling up and down hills, and generally trying to measure accurately the farmer's holding. Coconut tree plantings, cocoa plantings, and small food plots found on a block were obviously not planted with this work in mind.

By the time one or two such blocks were completed, one was totally exhausted from the effort and from the humidity and sun. But you still had to walk back to the village or wherever you were going to spend the night.

This physical adjustment to the climate and to working in the rugged terrain required a supreme effort. It was largely a matter of just grinning and bearing it. I did the best I could as did Dave and Charlie in their respective situations. None of us had an easy time of it as the working conditions were the same. We had wanted very much to get out into the field, to see what it was really like and this was it. There was no turning back now, unless we wanted to give up the whole idea. No one had said that the grand adventure of being a Peace Corps Volunteer would be easy. But then we didn't know how hard it would be either.

I recall the very first time that I went out to learn the census work firsthand. It was only a week or two after we had arrived in Savusavu and Dave was not feeling well that day, so I took his place. I went out to a farmer's holding just outside Savusavu somewhere with Pita Ralaca, Dave's co-worker on the census.

The day was partly cloudy, as most South Pacific days are, with a bright sun and high humidity. The farm we were to measure that day was a typical coconut plantation, however small. The thing that stands out most in my mind is wading through a swamp to get to the coconut grove and then struggling around the perimeter counting off the measurement. Then we had to make an estimate of the density of coconut trees per acre, so we had to measure off one acre and wade through the swampy muddy mess again to count the trees in the one-acre plot.

After locating and marking the land holding on the aerial photograph, we were ready to count the density of coconut trees per acre, using one sample acre as a guide.

"Well Pita, "I said, "what shall we do now?" I wasn't exactly giving the orders here…I was waiting for them.

"We should plot out one acre here and count the trees," replied Pita.

"How shall we do that?" I asked again.

"Well, you pace off that direction and I'll go this direction and we'll make an acre," Pita said abruptly.

Since he sounded like he knew what he was doing, I did like he said. I plowed through that swampy grove again, pacing off my sides of our sample acre.

"OK Pita, now what?" I hollered when I came to the end.

"Let's start counting the trees and see how close we come to each other's total," he shouted back.

So off we went again, wading through the grove, sometimes tripping and sinking in muck over our ankles, all just to count some coconut trees. My boots and socks were soon soaked through and clothing speckled with mud. It was quite an introduction to my new job.

To say the least, it was a very humbling experience because I really didn't know what I was doing. I couldn't understand the language that well, though Pita spoke excellent English. The terrain too was just very difficult to work in. The sheer difficulty of moving through the swampy wetland coupled with my general disorientation, not to mention the heat and humidity, left me totally exhausted at the end of the day. But for some reason, that very first day I spent working on the census was particularly significant. Perhaps it was because it brought home the fact that I really was out in the bush now, seeing what the real Fiji was like.

A particularly significant note from my journal of March 6, 1968, reads:

"...Nawi...by the way, I think I am beginning to understand why Fijians are supposed to be easy going and indifferent to too much hard work. It gets so darned hot here nobody has the energy to get out and work in the bush. Walking is hard enough on the roads here. But cutting through the bush would be, and is, tough going."

Another particularly significant and meaningful event happened at Nawi during the time I was located there. Having completed a few weeks of the census work, I was getting familiar with the villages and learning more about the language and culture. I was becoming more confident and used to my situation.

One of the young Nawi famers, named Tony, invited me to visit his newly cleared block of land. Since nothing else was planned that day I accepted. After an early breakfast, we started off down the road to his block of land, some three miles away.

We arrived at Tony's block of land after the leisurely walk from Nawi. His 30-acre block is situated in the interior of the island peninsula that makes up this southeastern tip of Vanua Levu. It fronts the road, but the terrain is quite hilly and rugged.

The government subsidized the farmers for clearing their land and planting coconuts, the main cash crop in this area of Fiji. The government had decided on a monetary subsidy system to encourage the villagers to develop their land. Otherwise the land would lay idle and the villagers would tend to stay in their villages and follow the traditional ways of subsistence farming.

"You know John," Tony said to me, "I've been working hard to clear this land and to plant coconuts."

"Yes, I can see that you've done much work here Tony," I answered.

"I have cleared it all by myself with just my axe and knife. It has take (sic) me a long time," he said proudly. "You know John," he continued, "you are the first 'vavalagi' to visit my block of land. It makes me happy to have you come here."

"Well, I'm glad I came," I said, "you've done much work here to make your farm productive." I was trying to sound supportive.

"Well, yes, but I have a dream. One day I hope my land will be covered with coconut trees and that they will bear plenty of copra. I want to send my children to school and to build a wooden house. I also hope that maybe one day I will have enough money to buy one small truck. It would be so nice to have a truck to drive and deliver my vegetables to the market in Savusavu," Tony explained.

Tony indeed had big dreams for his farm.

You must appreciate the efforts that these people go through to work here. Considering the hot stifling climate and the lack of machines to do their work, it is a wonder they get anything accomplished at all. Tony had cleared his 30-acre block all by hand labor, quite an achievement in itself.

Tony had a small bamboo hut with a corrugated metal roof on his block. He told me that at times he would come down to his block with his wife and child and spend a few days at a time working on his farm.

It is very difficult to do this, especially for the village-oriented Fijian. It is difficult to cope with the loss of social interaction and the support of family and friends in the village. This plus the fact of an unreliable water supply at the block and the meagerly furnished house force the average Fijian back to his village and the security and relative comfort it provides. Pioneering a block of land in the bush is a very harsh and lonely existence.

Tony had brought with him that day a can of corned beef, a luxury for these poor Fijians. He had probably paid about $.50 for it at the village store, paying for it with money he had received from his family's or clan's share of copra, dried coconut meat. This can of corned beef was our lunch.

Tony worked around the block, clearing brush and weeds, after making a fire to start cooking our lunch. I went along with him, pulling a weed here and there. We talked much, mostly in broken English, mixed with Fijian, as Tony had an elementary school education from the Catholic mission over on Taveuni Island, just across the bay.

We continued talking during our lunch break of corned beef stew with greens and tavioka root, followed by tea. I've often thought of that visit since then. It was one of those special moments from which I learned much. I learned just how much a villager must go through in order to develop his land, what difficulties he must endure and how hard he really must work.

I learned that there is great pressure on these Fijian villagers to change and to conform at the same time. The government tells them to change by leaving their villages with the protective shield of traditional living and to develop their land. At the same time, the village tells them to conform by staying in the village and following the traditional life-style of communal living.

For a young man like Tony, who is being pulled in both directions at once, it is a difficult choice. His village tells him to remain traditional and the government tells him to modernize and progress. Tony is walking a middle road, trying his best to develop and change but clinging to what he can of his village background. These young farmers like Tony must be given credit for achieving what they have under extremely difficult conditions.

During those first few weeks in the field, we experienced and learned much. We learned just what it took to survive in the bush and in the jobs we had. There was certainly nothing glamorous about what we were doing. It was simply dirty tough demanding work. We frequently reflected on our very inadequate training in Hawai`i. Of course, no training could substitute for the actual experience of being out in the real Fiji, learning the language and culture, getting to know the people, and learning the work we were sent to do. Experience was our teacher and a tough one at that.

One of those early days when I operated out of Nawi, I walked over to Navonu development area with Josefa and another young fellow from Nawi. Navonu was not a village but an area of newly developing blocks or homesteads located about three miles down the Hibiscus Highway from Buca Bay. From Nawi, this would be some seven to nine miles, one way.

We left Nawi early in the morning, followed the coastal foot path rather than cutting inland via the road. The coastal route saved some difficult hilly walking and it saved on time and distance as well. We arrived at Navonu in mid-morning and located a farm to measure. We finished by early afternoon despite the extreme heat and difficulty of the terrain we covered.

Measuring the blocks of land was not easy. Pacing off the small food gardens proved very difficult as one had to struggle through dense vines and foliage to get to the cleared food plots. The heat and humidity, increased by the dense jungle foliage, made a steam bath out of the area. Locating the whole block on an aerial photograph was the easiest part of the job. Actually pacing out the garden plots was agonizing to say the least.

At any rate, we completed the blocks at Navonu for that day. Already exhausted from the efforts, we began our trek back up the road to Buca Bay and Nawi. Along the way, we stopped and visited briefly with people in Vunikura or those who lived along the road. One often stopped just to pass the time of day while passing through the area. This, of course, provided a chance to rest along the way.

The journal of April 23, 1968, notes:

"...what a day this was, Josefa and I walked clear over to Navonu, past Loa, to see one lousy holder. My Lord! We must have walked 14-16 miles all together. Luckily, we got a ride in a PWD truck the last five miles to Nawi. But I am still sore, aching, and dead tired."

So, for the day we had hiked several miles in addition to enumerating the holding. It was a full day of work and then some. But this was to be a somewhat typical day on the agriculture census.

There was an amusing part to this episode the next day in Nawi. Because we had worked hard at Navonu, we decided to rest this day in Nawi. After awaking for morning tea, I went back to the bure which I shared with Tui. He was away at the time working elsewhere and one of the boys from the village, Joe Bibi, was keeping me company.

Both Joe and I fell back into our beds to sleep, still drawn out by our long hike of the day before. Along about mid-morning, a Land Rover came roaring into Nawi and drove right up to my bure. It was the Agriculture Department Land Rover with my friend Ram, the driver. He was bringing a visitor to see me, none other than the Deputy Director of Peace Corps-Fiji, Fred Schierer. I had barely gotten awake and up and out of my bed when Fred bounded in and announced, "Aha! I caught you in the sack, sleeping on the job!"

Indeed, he had. Well, we all had a good laugh over that. After explaining why he caught me in the sack, I managed to gain Fred's sympathy. It was not really an embarrassing situation because I certainly felt we warranted a day off from work. In fact, I was just simply too exhausted to go anywhere that day. I had heard that Fred was going to be on Vanua Levu trying to visit us guys. Peace Corps administrators were making the rounds and checking up on how we Volunteers were doing at our various posts. I had figured that he would not come on this particular day, if at all. I guessed wrong.

At any rate, Fred stayed for lunch and was a real celebrity in Nawi and especially for the family that took care of me. Fred was fond of wearing a cowboy hat and boots, which most of us can readily accept. But to the Fijians, well, anybody wearing a cowboy hat and boots and was big and husky like Fred, just had to be a genuine, certified, born-in-the-saddle cowboy. He certainly made an impact with the village folks that day.

To understand this, you must understand the mentality of the average Fijian villager. This guy had little formal education and exposure beyond his immediate village. What education he had was from the village or mission primary school. What cultural or social exposure he had otherwise to the world may have been in the form of an occasional movie in one of the provincial towns. These movies were nothing spectacular or outstanding or even of recent vintage. For the most part, the movies Fijians had been exposed to were the cheap "B" movies of the 40's, 50's, and 60's. Most of them had themes favoring war, love, cowboys and Indians, or a combination thereof. Unfortunately, as we came to understand, the typical Fijian conception of American culture and Americans in general was based on what they had seen in the movies.

Thus, it was no surprise then to have Fred come walking into the isolated village of Nawi and to have the people immediately assume that the heroic "American cowboy" had come to their village. What else could they have concluded?

When Fred left that afternoon, I was left to answer many questions about my "cowboy" friend who came to see me. I had a most difficult time convincing them that Fred was not really a cowboy. At any rate, the incident gave me a little more perspective into the Fijian mind. It was only the beginning of my long attempt to dispel myths and rumors concerning American cultural phenomena such as whether cowboys still shoot Indians and so on.

The agriculture census was off to a start in Cakaudrove Province. We Volunteers, in our roles as supervisors, worked closely with the seven or eight enumerators scattered throughout the province. We were "boso levu" (big boss) to these men, but during these first few weeks as we learned our work, we seldom felt like bosses. In fact, there were often times when we took direction and learned from our co-workers, such was the situation that we were so unfamiliar with what we were doing. Time and experience had a way of reversing our roles whereby after we gained a better working knowledge of the language and the census-surveying work, we took more of a leadership role.

The sheer amount of work to be done tended to confound the best of our efforts. In my area of Buca Bay alone there were well over 300 farms to be surveyed and measured. Multiply this by six or seven other districts in the province and our whole team was confronting a formidable task of completing the census in the timetable of one calendar year as planned.

Realizing this and considering that Cakaudrove Province is one of the most isolated backward areas of Fiji, with poor communications and transportation systems, and it indeed became a fearsome challenge to someone who knew the land, people, culture, and language. To inexperienced young foreigners on their first real working job, it was an almost insurmountable task. Luckily, we didn't realize much of this; otherwise we may have been frightened off by the rather grim reality of the situation.

The problems of working on the agriculture census have already been described, particularly those of acclimatization for us PCVs, bushwhacking in the jungle, and so on. The personal adjustments each of us would make individually were numerous as well, ranging from language, culture and food, to just learning to feel comfortable in a foreign environment and just getting to know one's way around. These, of course, were personal things that we had to cope with on an individual basis.

One problem that each of us did have in common was transportation. The nature of our work required that we travel around the respective assigned districts of the province quite a lot. This presented unique problems depending on where it was we needed to go. For even though the eastern section of the province was served by a road, the Hibiscus Highway ran from Savusavu to Buca Bay, fully 75 percent of the province was accessible only by boat or by walking via coastal trails or jungle paths over the hills and mountains of the island's interior.

We quickly learned that the transportation system, be it taxi cabs, busses, boats, or airplanes, operated on a distinctly Fijian timetable—infrequent at best and unreliable at worst. It seemed that there was always a man here or there who operated a boat or car for hire. Often, it was an Indian man who owned the car or boat and hired out his vehicle accordingly. Each of us learned who to contact or where to go in the areas we worked in order to arrange our transportation.

But often, the mere act of arranging transportation did not guarantee that it would be there at the time and place agreed upon. We often found out that waiting for a boat to go up Natewa Bay or across Savusavu Bay or around Buca Bay meant waiting, and waiting, and waiting. Often waiting for a boat meant spending another night, unplanned, in a village or settlement. It often threw work schedules off. This soon became the rule and not the exception. It was a difficult thing to tolerate. Again, we learned to adjust to the concept of "island time."

The journal for December 13, 1968, aptly notes:

"Typical of Fiji...you spend half of the time just waiting to go somewhere. But at least it doesn't bother me like it used to. It's just one of the many things that I've learned to put with since I've been here."

And another entry from April 29, 1969, seems to exemplify the constant battle against the concept of time and the idea of waiting that is so indigenous to the South Pacific:

"...Now sitting here at Nutuvu waiting for a ride back to Tukavesi. Still reading Michener and he talks about 'waiting, the constant waiting in the South Pacific.' It's really true. Sure doing a lot of it today."

As for types of transportation, there was variety. As much as possible, we made use of agriculture department Land Rovers. These are the British version of a jeep. They are probably a better built and more dependable vehicle than the jeep. The only problem we had with the Land Rover was that there was usually only one available, two at the most, for the entire province. One was often out of commission due to careless accidents caused by department staff that shouldn't have been driving in the first place.

Of particular use to my area since I had access, were the local taxi cabs owned and driven mostly by Indians. In Buca Bay, there were two such men who owned the small Australian built sedans. They often made daily round trips to Savusavu and around Buca Bay at nominal fees. It was usually $.80 to $1.00 for a one-way ride between Buca Bay and Savusavu. One made arrangements for the ride by contacting the drivers ahead and making reservations for a certain time and day. Trips had to be planned carefully and transportation given full consideration.

The cab ride was quite luxurious in comparison to the reliable old jungle bus. The jungle bus, as we called them, was in fact a stripped-down truck bed and frame with a bus built on top. It had open windows with canvas side flaps for rainy days and provided a wrenching, gut-busting, dusty ride. It was built to seat maybe 24 people comfortably but usually carried twice that many on the fifty-mile trip between Buca Bay and Savusavu. The bus itself was painted in bright orange, green, blue, and yellow, or a combination of those colors. The village people were equally colorful in their mixture of languages, clothes, bundles of foodstuffs, and so on, that they managed to carry with them on the bus.

The bus stopped frequently up and down the highway to load and unload passengers and cargo. To ride up or down the Hibiscus Highway on the jungle bus was to experience a real living part of Fiji. It was a chance to rub elbows with the village and country people, the real Fijians. The trip itself, though physically tiring and uncomfortable—three hours over a bumpy, hilly, dusty road—provided a close look at Fiji and its people. Besides it was cheaper than taking a taxi too, only $.50 for the trip from Buca Bay to Savusavu.

I will say this about the jungle busses; they were fairly regular and generally reliable, unlike most other transportation options available to us. Not once in my entire two years in Cakaudrove did I encounter a delay due to mechanical breakdown on one of the busses, not even a flat tire. Now that is a record of some sort.

One amusing aspect of riding the jungle busses was that we were constantly amazed at the cargo the local folks would carry. In addition to the village people, the back of the bus and lower storage racks carried an amazing variety of goods, from fruit and vegetables, roots, baskets, mats, to live chickens and even an occasional pig. It all added to the color, chaos, and fun of riding on that bus. What a way to go!

The difficulties in trying to get around Cakaudrove by boat were especially trying at times. Here again it is worth noting that much of our work required us to cross water at one point or another. And of course, this required boat transportation.

The most common forms of boat transportation were small open boats with an outboard motor, locally called "putt putts" because of the distinct "putt putt" sound they usually made. Another common type of boat was the launch, a sort of Fijian cabin cruiser. Typically, it was around 20-25 feet long with an enclosed cabin on top. It was usually powered by an ancient smoke belching diesel engine and steered by a stick rudder.

The Buca Bay-Taveuni Island launch was such a typical boat. On a calm day, it probably had a top speed of seven or eight knots which severely taxed the ancient wooden craft and the fragile old power plant. The Indian boat owner would stand at the helm with one foot on the steering stick/rudder and would lean out to the side while sighting his course across Buca Bay. In one hand he often had a nylon fishing line used to troll while crossing the bay. Usually he landed a couple of fish of the small tuna variety.

Buca Bay was usually a safe passage but could prove treacherous on a stormy day. The many times that I crossed the bay there was only once that it was fairly rough.

The journal entry for March 22, 1968, notes:

"...finally got a boat back to Vanua Levu from Taveuni and then by Land Rover to Savusavu for the weekend again. What a hell of a ride in that boat today. The waves were really big and tossed the old boat around a lot. But made it safely."

Our work was not entirely without its elements of danger, especially when it came to riding boats across rough seas known to harbor sharks. Many of these old boats were probably unfit to be on the water but that did not deter those who ran them or needed to ride them.

One instance of real danger that turned out to be a harrowingly close call comes to mind. Fortunately, no one was injured nor were any of us Volunteers involved.

Dave was traveling via the agriculture outboard boat across Savusavu Bay to the Wailevu area in December 1968. With him were two of the census workers, Pita Relaca and Filomone Ratumainaceva. They had just put Dave off at the village of Dreketi and were out in the bay underway again. On board was a 50-gallon drum of gasoline.

Suddenly, the engine began sparking and sputtering dangerously. Filomone, a quick thinking British Army veteran, tore loose the gas line and both he and Pita dove overboard. They thought sure there would be an explosion.

Luckily there wasn't that day. But the possibility of a tragic accident was always there, especially in very remote isolated areas. Fortunately, none of us ever met any such accident during our term of service.

Another type of over water transportation was the outrigger canoe. This was unique to the Polynesian people of Kioa Island in Buca Bay and to the Banabans of Rabi Island. The Fijians of Vanua Levu had long ago lost the art of building canoes. Few areas of Fiji still use them.

However, the Kioans used them extensively, perhaps because their small island had no roads and no other type of transportation system except walking. They also were great fishermen and were often seen plying the waters of Buca Bay in search of fish.

An outrigger canoe is basically a hollowed-out log with a stabilizing pole lying parallel to the canoe body. The stabilizer or outrigger is attached to the main hull by other small poles and tied in place with coconut fiber twine. The outrigger allows the canoe to remain upright in the water. Without it the canoe would be unbalanced and would not remain upright.

The Kioans went everywhere in their canoes, all around Buca Bay. I recall fondly one memorable trip I made in an outrigger across Buca Bay to Kioa. The son of Nellie Lefuka, the leader of Kioa, came and picked me up one day to take me to see Kioan dancing and attend a village festival. We crossed Buca Bay, some three or four miles to Kioa, in an outrigger canoe. I had to help paddle and for me it was really quite an experience. Here I was a kid from Iowa, in the South Pacific, paddling an outrigger canoe. What an experience! I returned to Tukavesi in the same manner. During several trips to Kioa, I had a couple of other chances to ride in the outrigger canoes.

The other main type of over water transportation was the classic old inter-island trading steamer or copra boats. These small ships plied the island waters bringing the essential goods from the outside world to the most remote and isolated areas of the islands. In exchange, it took back to Suva the products of the islands, mainly copra (dried coconut meat), cocoa beans, and some cattle and occasional other locally produced goods.

The old Fijian Princess, a converted Japanese fishing boat, which originally brought us PCV's to Savusavu, was a typical example. Other Fijian copra boats of the era included the Ului Lakemba, the Ai Sokula, and for a while, the flag ship of the Fijian trading fleet, the regal Tui Lau.

The Tui Lau (King of Lau) was the largest and newest ship carrying cargo and passengers between the islands. Acquired in 1968 by the government of Fiji, she was put into service and operated for only a few months. In a tragic ending, the Tui Lau ran aground on a reef in, ironically, Lau, the eastern coral atolls of Fiji. The ship was a total loss, being broken up on the reef by the sea. Fortunately, all on board were rescued but Fiji lost the premier addition to her trading fleet at that time.

Dave, Charlie, and I were lucky enough to have made a voyage on the Tui Lau prior to her grounding on that Lauan reef. We rode to Suva from Savusavu on one of our early leaves. We decided to travel on the Tui Lau rather than the airplane, as we normally did when going on leave. That voyage on the Tui Lau was a memorable one. For us, it was most enjoyable, as we had a bed to sleep in on board, a shower, food, and the comforts of a real ocean liner. It was an overnight cruise to Suva and a most delightful way to travel. Along with the Fijian people, we grieved the tragic ending of the regal Tui Lau.

Although we didn't use air travel directly in our work on the agriculture census, we did use it often, usually to go on leave to Suva, the capital city. The local airline, Fiji Airways, was also referred to as Fiji Scareways. It certainly was no match for any international airline. Fiji Airways operated a somewhat regular flight schedule between Viti Levu, the main island, and Vanua Levu and Taveuni. It used 15-passenger, four prop, British made Heron aircraft. It also flew a couple of ancient but reliable DC-3s, the old "gooney bird" of World War II fame. The fleet was basically a bunch of venerable old puddle jumpers.

Fiji Airways served us well, proving to be usually reliable and safe, at least during our service in Fiji. The biggest problem we had was trying to control our pulse rate each time we boarded one of those fragile old birds. Our rates must have tripled each time.

It was quite a thrill however, to swoop and soar over the islands and atolls between Vanua Levu and Viti Levu when we were on our way to leave time. It was an exhilarating beginning to what was usually for us an exciting vacation in the big city.

Regardless of how we viewed or approached the transportation problem in the field on the job, it still boiled down to one thing in the end: walking. No matter what you did, walking was still the most reliable form of transportation in the province. We soon got used to the idea of walking and plenty of it. Even though we were transported via land, sea, or air, our work required us to walk, hike, charge, push, struggle, or in some way or another, traverse the land with our own two feet. Out in the field, on the job doing the agriculture census, it was the only way.

The bush country of Cakaudrove Province was not an easy place in which to get around. We learned through experience how to get around and have fun doing it. We learned as we did get around too. We learned the language more, we got more intimately involved with the people, and we came to appreciate and understand the problems these people faced on their road to progress.

For us, our work on the agriculture census was an introduction to the land, people, and culture of Fiji. Through our work, we learned what it was really like to live in the bush of Cakaudrove Province. We found that living in the bush could be both rewarding and discomforting.

CHAPTER 6

A PARAMOUNT CHIEF'S FUNERAL

From February through mid-May 1968, we learned how to get along in the bush country of Cakaudrove. It was in mid-May that we got a break in the form of the first Peace Corps conference in Suva.

This was a gathering with all our friends and fellow Volunteers, a chance to exchange stories, and a confirmation that we indeed were surviving the rigors of bush living. The conference gave the Peace Corps staff a chance to assess our adjustment and adaptation to our new jobs.

It was a welcome change of scene, allowing us to enjoy the luxurious delights that Suva had to offer namely bright lights, real food, booze, and partying. The entire visit lasted for a week or so and helped to rekindle our enthusiasm and morale. It was simply a great feeling to see a city again, to sleep in a good bed, enjoy hot showers, and other delights. It was the Peace Corps version of R&R.

Up to the time that we went to Suva that May, we were still involved in learning the work of the agriculture census. Also, we were still being immersed into Fijian culture. Things were just beginning to happen for us. We were just beginning to get a handle on our overall situation.

However, I was still without a permanent residence in my assigned area, Buca Bay. This was due to the Agriculture Department's mishandling of getting my housing built at the Tukavesi Agriculture Station.

So, I was dividing time between Savusavu, our provincial headquarters, Nawi at Buca Bay, and Taveuni Island to the east of Buca Bay. Since Paul had left Taveuni, I took over supervision of the census for that area. From March to May, I was constantly on the move between those areas. I spent little time in any one location.

Despite my efforts, the work production on the census slowed down somewhat. The progress and direction of the census work became a bit disorganized in Buca Bay due to my sometimes misguided and misdirected efforts. It was difficult to control the work on the census in the separate areas for which I was responsible. It was characteristic of the initial disorganization of our entire provincial census effort. Time and experience in the field helped to overcome these difficulties.

Being somewhat free to roam the eastern areas of the province at will had its advantages, however. I saw and experienced quite a lot during those first three or four months.

One of the most memorable experiences I had occurred in mid-March 1968, when I was in Nawi. The Paramount Chief of Cakaudrove, Tui Cakau, died. Culturally, it was a particularly important event in Fiji as Tui Cakau traditionally is a powerful tribal leader among the northern islands of Fiji.

I had spent the weekend of March 16-17 at James Makasiale's house in Savusavu, the Peace Corps Hotel, as we called it in those early days. On Sunday, the 17th, while preparing to return to Buca Bay and Nawi on Monday, word arrived of Tui Cakau's death in Suva. James, being a relatively high government officer, made immediate plans to attend the funeral on Taveuni Island, as did many other provincial government leaders in Savusavu. This was especially warranted since Tui Cakau was the Paramount Chief of Cakaudrove Province. Culturally and politically Tui Cakau was held in extremely high regard and most government leaders were duty bound to attend this important funeral.

The journal entry for Monday, March 18, 1968, notes:

"...returned to Nawi and picked up good clothes. Off to Taveuni for the big chief's funeral tomorrow. Waited for the boat at Buca Bay (Nutuvu landing) till 11:00PM. James Makasiale, the Roko (a local Fijian government leader), the D.O. (District Officer) and other government officials from Cakaudrove Province also going. Arrived at Somosomo, Taveuni, about 1:30AM the 19th."

I do not recall too much about the journey across the straits from Buca Bay to Taveuni. I do recall that I had a difficult time sleeping, that it was crowded on the boat, a large launch, and that we did arrive in the early morning hours of March 19th.

My journal for March 19, 1968, continues:

"...I am just sitting here in a bure in Somosomo waiting for the funeral to begin. They just brought the chief's body from Suva in a big boat, so it may not be too long. The only thing is that it's been raining all night and morning and I don't know what's actually going to happen."

After arriving on Taveuni, we went to the chiefly village of Somosomo, the home of Tui Cakau. I was put up in a bure with a young couple, Jim, and Sally Sorovakaca. Jim was a clerk at the Taveuni Agriculture Office and Sally was a teacher at the village school.

This was my first visit to their home, and they took me in with the usual Fijian welcome of hospitality. I had met Jim on an earlier visit to Taveuni with Big James. But since James had to attend other functions relating to Tui Cakau's funeral, he asked Jim and Sally to take me in, which they did willingly. It was the beginning of a warm friendship with this young Fijian couple, whom I returned to visit several times over the following months. Sally in fact, made the beautiful floral wreath which I was to present at Tui Cakau's funeral as the Peace Corps representative.

There were two major reasons why James wanted me to attend this funeral in the first place. First, culturally it was a big event. It was a rare chance to see some of the real color of Fijian culture, even on such a solemn occasion. Secondly, it would be terrific public relations for a representative of the American Peace Corps to be there. James, being the true Fijian and friend that he was to us, saw this event as an opportunity to gain exposure in both areas.

Since I was the one Volunteer who happened to be in Savusavu at the time, he asked me to go with him. Of course, both Dave and Charlie would have gone along had they been in town at the time. I happened to be in the right place at the right time, to take part in this rather significant event. At the time however, I was completely unaware of the cultural significance of the entire affair, including the role I would play as the sole representative of the Peace Corps at the funeral of one of Fiji's highest-ranking leaders.

It was during this time that Paul, our fourth Volunteer on Taveuni, was sick in the hospital. For that reason, he also was not able to take part in this important event, even though it took place in his territory. In fact, during my visit to Taveuni that week, I visited Paul a couple of times at the hospital.

The funeral of Tui Cakau took place in his village of Somosomo. His coffin was borne by Fijian warriors dressed in full traditional battle regalia, up the hill overlooking the village. Thousands of Fijians had gathered in Somosomo to take part in this important event and to pay their respects to Tui Cakau. The Fijian warriors continuously blew the conch shells, signaling the death of a chief and the royal women wailed through the night and day continuously, expressing their grief and sadness. The entire village was covered with a very gloomy atmosphere, accentuated with a heavy overcast sky and the continuous drenching rain that fell without interruption.

The funeral was a very solemn and dignified affair, attracting the very elite of Fiji's tribal and governmental leaders. Inasmuch as I was relatively new to Fiji's culture, I did not fully understand the significance of the entire event until later. Perhaps in fact, this was just as well; otherwise the role I played may have made me nervous and apprehensive.

On Tuesday, March 19, the day of the funeral, I made my way up to the chiefly house situated on a hill overlooking Somosomo village. Coconut groves surrounded the village with the blue-gray Pacific stretching out to the horizon and the island of Vanua Levu and Buca Bay to the west. As to the plan laid out by James, I was accompanied up the hill by Jim, the fellow I was staying with and carried the flower wreath his wife made for me to present.

It was mid-morning with a gentle rain falling. Hushed crowds of glum looking Fijians lined either side of the roadway up to the house where Tui Cakau lie in state. Many ventured up closer to the chief's house, trying to gain a better vantage point. However, the Fijians, in the traditional spirit, did not attempt to overstep accepted boundaries in recognition of the strict taboos held between the common people and their chiefly leaders.

I was dressed in what formal clothing I had at the time. This included a dark colored sports jacket, white shirt and dark tie, dark pants, and shoes. It was not exactly a mourning outfit, but it was the best I could do. I had picked these up upon reaching Nawi on the trip to Buca Bay from Savusavu the day before.

As we wound our way up the road to Tui Cakau's house it became increasingly apparent that something big was in the air. Up to now, I was totally unprepared for the events that were soon to unfold.

Jim, who was only a couple of years older than me, served as my escort all the way up to the immediate house grounds. He became increasingly nervous as we neared the house, apparently sensing and perhaps fearing the entire scene himself. As we came up the last rise in the road and entered the house grounds, it became clear why Jim was so nervous and apprehensive.

The sound of the conch shells being blown, the wailing of the Fijian women, crying over the death of their chief, and the sight of a full contingent of royal Fijian warriors dressed in full traditional battle gear, war clubs and spears at the ready, faces blackened for battle, was enough to make anyone fearful of just what was going to happen.

Jim, serving as my interpreter, was scared stiff of proceeding any further. We were approached by one of the Fijian warriors who seemed to oversee things, sort of a master of ceremonies.

The spokesman asked Jim, "May I be of service to you?" in polite but serious Fijian.

Jim nervously replied, "This gentleman is here to present his respects on behalf of the United States Peace Corps."

The spokesman said, "Well, we are almost ready to proceed with the procession, but let me check inside the house. Wait here, please."

The Fijian spokesman turned and walked to the house. Jim and I were left to stand there, all alone, confronting the contingent of armed Fijian warriors guarding the chiefly premises. Naturally, I was scared myself. I had no idea what was going on as I could not understand much Fijian at that time.

The Fijian spokesman returned and said, "Please, you may enter the house to pay your respects and then join the distinguished guests afterwards."

With that, Jim translated, and said, "I will see you later." He quickly vanished into the nearby crowd.

In translating, Jim explained to me that we were kind of late in arriving there and that they were soon to bring the chief's body down the hill for burial. The other government officials and high tribal leaders from all over Fiji had already paid their respects and were all gathered under a shelter house off to the side of the chief's house. They were all waiting to follow the Fijian warriors as they bore the body of Tui Cakau down the hill for burial.

Since I was the sole representative of the American Peace Corps, I was allowed entry into the house to pay my respects. This was an honor and a privilege as not many people could enter the chief's house.

As was custom, I removed my shoes and entered the house, amidst a very rigid atmosphere, pierced by the wail of the women. I was taken into the parlor where Tui Cakau's coffin was wrapped in pandanus mats according to tradition. I placed my wreath and stood before the coffin and paid my respects. The Fijian spokesman accompanying me informed those in the house as to whom I was representing.

I exited through the same front door and was asked by the spokesman to join the other government officials and tribal leaders who stood waiting. This I did gladly, relieved to be out of the view of everyone.

However, the real significance of the event dawned on me when I realized I was now standing in the presence of Ratu Mara, the Chief Minister and head of government, Ratu George Cakobau, the traditional King of Fiji, and many of the cabinet ministers as well as high tribal leaders from all over Fiji, It was indeed esteemed company to be in. And here I was, just a lowly Peace Corps Volunteer who had been in the country barely two months. I then realized that I had just served as an unofficial representative of the United States at an especially important Fijian cultural and political event. I was a little proud of that.

It was not long before the Fijian warriors removed the body of their chief from the house. They carried the coffin down the hill to the burial place amidst the blowing of conch shells and the continuous wailing of the women. The group of government and tribal leaders I was with followed the warrior guards down the hill and the commoners followed us in procession. People lined both sides of the road and stooped to their knees and clapped three times in the Fijian custom as Tui Cakau passed them for the last time.

Upon reaching the burial place, the body was lowered into a pandanus mat lined grave. Traditional Fijian chants were sung by the warrior guards and by other Fijian dignitaries. Tui Cakau was lowered to his resting place with all the pomp and ceremony accorded to a Fijian high chief.

It was here that the rain stopped until Tui Cakau was buried. But it began again as soon as all formalities were completed at the grave site. From there, I found Jim again and returned to his house in the village of Somosomo.

The journal for March 19, 1968, notes:

"...well, I was the only representative of the Peace Corps, so in fact I was representing the USA also. I presented a wreath in Peace Corps' name and was honored to stand with the highest chiefs and government officials. I was also somewhat frightened by the occasion, but I didn't blow my cool. I think I represented the USA and the Peace Corps quite well. At least I hope so.

A few of the people said I did a fine job. It was quite an honor really to be in the same group as that of the Chief Minister, Ratu Mara, and the rest of the government officials. I must say I feel quite proud of myself and the way I performed. At least I hope I made a good impression.

This has been quite a memorable experience for me, the first and probably only time that I'll serve as an emissary or representative for such an event."

The weather on Taveuni continued rainy and windy through the entire week. We were not able to catch a boat back across Buca Bay until Friday and then travelled via Land Rover on back down to Savusavu. So, we had spent the entire week on Taveuni. I did not fully comprehend the significance of the affair until afterwards when James explained some things in more detail.

The journal for March 22, 1968, notes:

"...Guess I made a good impression on James with my attendance at the funeral this week. So maybe I helped the American and Peace Corps image a little. He said a few good words to me anyway this evening."

So again, our good friend and mentor, James Makasiale, proved to be extremely helpful. Without my knowing it, he gave me the opportunity of a lifetime to participate in a very real and important cultural event of Fiji as well as a chance to build the image of myself as a Volunteer and the image of the entire Peace Corps group in Fiji. It was just one way among many that James was to help us out and prove to be a real friend.

Looking back on the experience now, I feel quite proud to have served as the unofficial representative of the Peace Corps and the United States. I never received any official recognition for my efforts because it was a purely Peace Corps type of experience, people to people. That was the role I am most proud of playing.

CHAPTER 7

SURVIVAL IN THE BUSH

Toward the end of March 1968, for various reasons Paul transferred from Taveuni to Viti Levu, the main island. This left the Cakaudrove Team (as we became known) one man short with just Dave Reed, Charlie Matthews, and me. The large task facing us, conducting the agriculture census for the province, was immediately made larger and even more formidable.

Since Taveuni Island is adjacent to Buca Bay, I inherited that area for supervision along with the lone census field man there. This action did give me further opportunity to travel around the islands, to experience more, and to learn more about Fiji in this early period as we learned how to survive in the bush.

The first major holiday we celebrated in Fiji was Easter, 1968. I was still located in Nawi and was invited to accompany the people to Wairiki Mission on Taveuni. The Catholic mission was situated across the Somosomo Straits opposite the southeastern point of the Buca Bay peninsula, some six or eight miles from Nawi. The village, being predominately Catholic, planned a trip to Wairiki for Easter.

Since it was a major holiday and much fun and food were in the offing, I decided to go along with them. Little did I know how enjoyable the experience would be.

We arrived on the heavily laden village boat, Kalokalo (The Star), at Wairiki in the evening of Good Saturday, April 13th. I do not recall how many people were on the small craft, but it was probably dangerously overloaded with people, baggage, and food. I was welcomed to the mission by Father O'Neil and the Marist Brothers and Sisters who staffed the mission school. I received the royal treatment and was invited to stay in the old mission rectory itself.

My journal notes on April 13, 1968:

"...staying a room of which the building must be a hundred years old..."

The accommodations were Spartan but then one's whole lifestyle in Cakaudrove was too.

It has always been my belief that I was posted to Buca Bay for a specific reason. That was because I am a Catholic as were many of the villages in the Buca Bay district as well as on Taveuni. I have always felt that I was given the assignment because I would have this factor in my favor. No one ever told me this directly, but I have always felt that this was a significant factor in my placement at Buca Bay. As it turned out, this was to my advantage and did in fact aid my acceptance by the people of the Buca Bay area.

At the Easter celebration at Wairiki, I joined the villages for Midnight Mass at the mission church. It was a very impressive gathering of hundreds of people, dressed in their finery, singing Fijian hymns.

After Mass, the people gathered at the meeting hall for a huge yaqona drinking session and dance. The yaqona session and dance were sponsored by the mission school to help raise funds for their projects.

The dance was a rousing success as many young people from all around attended.

I did my share of yaqona drinking and dancing with the "gone yalewa," the young girls. I recall also, my good friend from Nawi, Joe Bibi, calling me outside in between dances to tank up on some cheap dark "Overpoof" rum he had purchased at the general store.

Of course, a Fijian dance was not a dance if the fellows were not tanked up a little. So, Joe and I downed the rum with water. I remember clearly, the two of us squatting under some trees near the church, using an old teacup to mix the rum and water and taking turns passing the cup around. What a way to get high! And then we headed back to the dance inside to work up a sweat dancing and work off the rum. As usual, the dance continued until the early morning hours.

On Easter Sunday, after morning Mass again, I was invited by the nuns to dinner. A journal entry for Easter Sunday, 1968, explains it all very well:

"...This afternoon I was treated to an unbelievable dinner by the nuns here at the Mission. I accompanied Fathers O'Neil and Jone and the Brothers here to Easter dinner. Man! I have not seen so much food since I do not know when! Meat, potatoes, rice, peas and carrots, stewed tomatoes, all kinds of pastries and jello for dessert! I can really say this whole trip has been worth it all just for that one meal. It was beautiful!"

It was things like this that really helped us over some difficult times. The entire trip over Easter to Wairiki was beneficial. I ate well, better anyway than I did at the village level. I thoroughly enjoyed the company of the priests, brothers, and nuns at the mission, to talk with someone on my own level for a change. And in turn, I got to better know the people with whom I was living and working. In all it was a beneficial weekend trip.

The journal entry for April 16th. describes my feelings at the time:

"...I came back with the Nawi people and had a fun-filled ride back. I think I am really starting to settle in with these people here. They are really great people and really accept me among them. Oh! The joys of singing with them on a boat ride back from Taveuni. The joking and carrying on, all in fun. The fantastic beauty of watching a golden red sunset with Vanua Levu in the background and on and on. So many real meaningful moments that I am only now beginning to realize. I really think that I am going to miss these people here in Nawi when I go to Tukavesi. So many things are starting to fall in line, at least the part of the experience that is just getting to know the people, talking, laughing, learning, and really loving them."

Much of our survival in the bush was dependent upon making ourselves known to the people and in turn getting to know them and adapting to the environment. This is what our early experiences tended to accomplish, making ourselves known throughout the areas we worked in.

Dave Reed aptly put it this way in one of his letters dated July 10, 1968, to his family in Maryland:

"...Right now, I am lying on the floor Fijian style. I am in the village of Nukubalavu (wide sand). Outside it is a full moon. It is fantastically beautiful. The nuku (sand) is balavu (wide). The coconut trees are silhouetted already into the sky. The moonlight cuts a simmering swath through the gentle sea (waitui) near the village (koro)."

Dave continued in the same letter with some ideas on being in a Fijian village:

"...Culture shock is the Peace Corps jargon for feeling very out of place in another way of life. It is easy to get it in Nukubalavu since no one can speak English. So, for my free time, I brought along <u>Mr. Clemens and Mark Twain</u>. It's an excellent book and also fits Margaret Mead's bushwhacking advice: 'Take a thick book along.'"

The experiences we had, such as my Easter trip to Wairiki and even Tui Cakau's funeral, helped to gain recognition for us and improved our image. We used to like to call these experiences "hanging loose with the people," for in fact that is what we did. We came down to the Fijians' level and showed them that we could live as they do. With these experiences we became more and more accepted for what we were: three young men who wanted to live among the people and be accepted by them, to share experiences with them, to learn from them, and perhaps teach them a few things as well.

If nothing else, we helped to dispel any false assumptions or misconceptions the Fijians may have had about "kai vavalagis" or foreigners, especially Americans. We showed them that we could come and live among them.

In working and living so closely with our host Fijians, over time we gathered our own impressions of the country and the people. Excerpts from Dave's letters to his family reflect how deeply these impressions were on us.

Dave's letter of October 23, 1968 notes:

"...I associate so much with people on the bottom that I rarely sense colonialism. I usually just feel that I am a PCV working somewhere in the world. I rarely meet Europeans and usually speak Fijian with farmers with a 5th. grade education. Fiji does not have the stealthy atmosphere of an oppressive society. People work, suffer, laugh, and live as they do all over the world. It is actually a pretty good place that could be a hell of a lot better."

And another of Dave's letters of November 25, 1968, notes:

"...I often feel my letters home don't really convey what it's really like here. It's really impossible I guess to describe three hour 'talanoas' (yarns), with men who were born and will die with 'sele levus' (machetes) in their hands, but I wouldn't trade the experience for all the movies and TV in the world."

During the first several weeks of adjustment to our respective living situations, Dave, Charlie, and I would get together to discuss our situations. Often there were specific experiences to relate to one another or things to discuss in general regarding being a Volunteer in Fiji.

In these early days, survival was much on our minds and of great concern to us all. As early March conversation that Dave had with our friend Big James helped somewhat to allay some of the fears we had.

"Well James, just how difficult is it...surviving in a village?" Dave asked apprehensively one day.

Big James answered by saying, "Aw Dave, don't you worry. Just be a nice guy huh? Just be a nice guy."

Dave always kept that in mind. It was simple advice from our good friend, Big James Makasiale.

I recall that we often discussed the topic of how Fijianized we were becoming. Because of our near total immersion in the local culture and our eager attempts to adopt and assume Fijian customs, language, food, etc., we were in fact losing, temporarily of course, our westernized habits and attitudes. When we finally came to realize this, it was quite amusing.

Dave put it rather aptly once when we discussed it, saying "You know, we're becoming regular bush apes up here in Cakaudrove." From that time on, we rather prided ourselves on becoming more Fijianized. There was no doubt in anybody's mind that we did achieve this with astonishing results.

By the end of our two years of service, we were well known in many parts of Cakaudrove Province, either through work related experiences or just because we had been to some far-out isolated village. We were the "Cakaudrove Team" to many of our cohorts, but to each other we were simply "bush apes."

One time when the three of us were together in Savusavu, the subject of our working together came up. Dave and I chided Charlie for his unfortunate luck in ending up having to work with us. Charlie is a black American from the south side of Chicago.

"Charlie," I said in mock seriousness, "what are you going to tell the folks back home after they find out you spent two years in Fiji working and living with two pieces of white trash (meaning Dave and myself)?"

"Well, you know," Charlie mused, "it may not be safe for me to go back to Chicago and tell them that!"

We all had a good laugh over that episode. It was typical of the camaraderie and esprit de corps that were felt for each other. We did make a good team and worked well together.

An example of our adoption of Fijian customs was the presentation of a "sevu" in each new village we visited. By Fijian custom, a first-time visitor to a village should present a "sevu" (gift), to the village headman or "turaga ni koro" (chief). The traditional gift was usually a pound or two of yaqona root.

Each of us routinely did this when we visited a village for the first time. Custom dictated that one who presents such a chiefly and honored gift to the village would in the future be welcomed into that village and always have a place to stay, food, and so on. Since our work on the census-survey required that we often stay in a village for several days, or make multiple visits to that village, the presentation of a "sevu" was a necessity.

Usually upon entering a village the bure of the "turaga ni koro" was sought out. Here, usually with a small throng of curious onlookers, the presentation of the sevu was formally made. The act was somewhat ceremonious and called for a specific procedure and proper method, all in Fijian with no English used.

Many times, in our early experiences, we were lucky to have another co-worker with us who made the presentation for us. This was a big help for us since we were limited in our language use during those early days.

Upon entering the bure where the presentation was made, all sat down, cross-legged on woven pandanus mats. The village headman or chief sat with his party and the visitors would sit opposite him. The sevu was pushed to the center of the floor toward the chief and the presenter clapped three times.

The presenter then gave a short speech saying to the effect that it was indeed a privilege and honor to visit the village and to work with the people here and that this small gift, totally inadequate, was a small token of gratitude. It was further hoped that cooperation would be extended to the visitors so that the work could be completed successfully.

In response, the chief or his spokesman, accepted the gift, pulling it toward him and said to the effect that the sevu was indeed a chiefly gift, a large gift, and it was accepted with appreciation and gratitude. A full welcome was extended to the visitors and cooperation was guaranteed.

The whole thing took only a few minutes but was strict and formal. Afterwards, everyone relaxed and smoked cigarettes or Fiji tobacco. Sometimes the yaqona was pounded immediately and mixed and drunk on the spot. This of course took up a few hours of time. Often however, the yaqona was saved until later, usually in the evening after the work was completed.

The highest point of presenting a sevu came however when we had to do it by ourselves. I recall specifically the time that I visited the small village of Koroko, about 15 miles north of Tukavesi on Buca Bay. I arrived at mid-day on the bus and stepped into the almost deserted village. Many people were out working on their gardens in the forest. I finally located the chief's son, who happened to run the village co-op store.

The people of Koroko had heard of me but did not really know me well. I told the fellow what I wanted to do so he led me to the chief's bure. He left me there, alone in the chief's bure while he fetched his wife, as many of the villagers as he could and a few children. With this curious throng of onlookers, I took out my sevu and proceeded to make the presentation.

It was probably the worst sevu presentation that was ever made, but if nothing else, it came from the heart. Being unskilled and not knowing what some of the ceremony meant, I did the best I possibly could. The people were totally impressed. For a "kai vavalagi" to come walking into their village and to present a chiefly sevu was a very brave and courageous act to the Fijians. They respected anyone who could do this, no matter how bad the actual presentation was. The fact that I was speaking their language and following their custom was a very flattering thing to these very humble and simple people. It immediately sealed for all time my good standing with this village.

As the time went on and we became adapted to our situations we became more conscious of our real roles as Volunteers. Of course, this varied with the individual. Each Volunteer probably saw his role in different ways based upon unique aspects and circumstances dependent upon his locale. As Volunteers we were assigned to teach or work for a specific governmental agency in Fiji. As such there were specific work roles to assume in any given assignment.

However, all assumed roles aside, there was the underlying role any Volunteer played to the hilt: that of a participant in a people to people program of international good will, sharing and understanding. This is what being in the Peace Corps was all about. Learning about another people and culture and perhaps having them learn something about you and your culture. This was the real meat of the Peace Corps experience.

Several instances of promoting these ideas of international good will, sharing and understanding were the times that I was asked to visit a village or mission school and speak to the school children. These occasions were thoroughly enjoyable for me as they gave me a chance to make myself and my reasons for being in Fiji better known. Besides, I loved all those grinning happy faces looking up at me.

One noteworthy school visit I made was up at Napuka Catholic Mission, at the north end of Buca Bay, about 20 miles from Tukavesi. I was on my initial visit to the Napuka area for the census work and was welcomed to the mission by Father Ramon Jarre, the pastor. The good father put me up at the mission while I worked the area. On my first afternoon there, he asked me to speak to the school children. I happily agreed. It turned out to be a stimulating experience.

The journal entry for November 20, 1968, notes:

"I gave a talk this afternoon to the school kids about America, me and the Peace Corps. Man! They really had some good questions—Viet Nam, cowboys and Indians, exports, and imports. Really surprising questions coming from kids. Anyway, I had a good time with them, and I think they enjoyed it also."

But it was not only the school kids with whom we interacted on visits to schools. We often had good interchange with the schoolteachers as well. It was on this same visit to Napuka school that I had a rewarding conversation with a couple of the schoolteachers there.

The journal for November 25, 1968, mentions that conversation:

"Last week while up at Napuka I was talking with the schoolteachers and the visiting teacher from Savusavu. They were asking questions about me and the Peace Corps and I was telling them about how we serve in the Corps, the many countries, etc. One teacher was quite surprised at the number of countries we serve in (more than 56 I think) and then the one teacher said, 'Oh, these people are helping the world.' This really struck me as, well, I felt proud and happy, and I will never forget her saying that. This woman was appreciative of what we have been doing here in Fiji, all of us PCVs, and she is pro-Peace Corps. So, it is moments like this that really make our stay here in Fiji meaningful. It makes one feel proud."

A further journal entry seems to underscore the importance of our relationship with the people. This entry is dated April 28, 1968:

"...Dave and I have had real good discussions and gripe sessions about our work here in Fiji, the Peace Corps ideal, etc. I think we have well agreed that this census work we are doing stinks. It just does not seem like we are able to do anything productively. And we also agree that our jobs of 'agriculture extension' are somewhat undefinable and we find it hard to understand our jobs here. But beside this somewhat pessimistic attitude we both feel that we are doing a fine job of getting to know the people and wining their friendship..."

In those early days, it was sometimes difficult to recognize results in the work we were doing. Given our situations, the circumstances of being in another culture, and our relative inexperience at what we were attempting to do, solid work results were difficult to see. Furthermore, it was difficult to see the results from our secondary roles as Volunteers, that of establishing rapport and excellent relationships with the people with whom we lived and worked.

The journal for May 23, 1968, notes:

Taveuni...I must say that I have killed a lot of time so far. I mean my situation here as far as my job goes is quite ambiguous. I really don't know what I am going to do next week. Will I move to a new location or what? I just don't know. This idea of being a Supervisor is great, but I feel that I should be doing something more. I spend too much time just doing nothing!"

The first several weeks of living in the bush in Cakaudrove were somewhat of a standoff. I personally liked the experience so far except for the overall disorganized unstructured work routine that was of necessity part of the job. Little did I know just what lay ahead over the next few months of beating the bush.

John off through the bush to work on the agriculture census.

John and his bure at Buca Bay, Tukavesi, Cakaudrove.

John and the jungle hills of Buca Bay, Cakaudrove, Fiji.

The infamous Cakaudrove Team: (L to R) John Penisten, Charles Matthews, Dave Reed, just back from Yacata Island

Charles and John about to board the Tui Lau in Savusavu.

Aerial view of Savusavu, Cakaudrove Province, Fiji

Downtown street scene, Savusavu, Fiji

Fijians gather around the yaqona bowl, Vanua Levu, Fiji.

James and Nuku Makasiale, our good friends from the early days in Cakaudrove and during our stay in Fiji.

Filo and Marama, my cultural and language mentors in Tukavesi from whom I learned so much.

Lolohae Waqatabu, head nurse at Savusavu Hospital, our good friend during our time in Savusavu.

Ping Ho's Cafe, the Peace Corps hangout in Savusavu, Fiji.

John's bure at the Tukavesi Agriculture Station, Buca Bay, Cakaudrove, Fiji.

CHAPTER 8

BEATING THE BUSH

My temporary location in Nawi village on Buca Bay finally got me out into the bush and into my census work. This is what I wanted. Finally, I was out in the country doing what I had come to Fiji to do.

Inasmuch as Nawi was the home base for Josefa, my field man for the census, it afforded the two of us to get to know each other better. Josefa was the son of the village chief. Nawi was a Catholic village and Josefa had been educated at Wairiki mission school over on Taveuni where all the village children were sent.

Josefa was a bright fellow, in his early 30's, and had been further educated through secondary school in New Zealand. He had in fact been in the seminary, training for the brotherhood. He spoke excellent English and was a hard worker. He was reliable and helped me improve in the language and explained many of the customs of Fiji.

One of the first field experiences I had with Josefa pointed out how Fijians were sizing us Volunteers up. We were tramping along the coast from Nawi to the village of Vunikura one afternoon where we were going to survey a couple of farms. We came to a small stream meandering through the jungle. It was not more than six feet wide and maybe several inches deep. Josefa stopped at the edge and stooped over.

"Here," he said, "get on my back."

"What for?" I asked.

"Well, so you don't get your feet wet," Josefa said humbly.

Well, it was sure a daring do case of whether I was the typical white colonialist who would use the humble native to keep his feet dry or a gung-ho, give 'em hell, Joe Peace Corps type, who didn't mind getting his feet wet at all.

I looked at Joe and he looked at me. I said, "You've got to be kidding!" as I charged on across the stream in my jungle boots.

That was one time that I thoroughly enjoyed getting my feet wet. Chalk up one small victory for the Peace Corps image. I felt proud. Josefa never offered to carry me across another stream.

There was another time that I did not really want to get my feet wet but did anyway. I was down in Buca village one afternoon measuring a couple of farms. Buca is only a mile below Tukavesi, my home base after I had relocated there.

I had bought a pair of Viet Nam combat boots at an Army surplus store in Hawai`i during training before leaving for Fiji. These boots were excellent for the type of bush work we had to do. The boots were admired by the Fijians, who were usually barefoot. There was a problem however and that was that on a small slippery log they could be a real hazard. That was what I discovered at Buca that day.

With a group of five or six villagers, we headed out to see one of the farmer's holdings. Along the way, we had to cross a stream 15-feet wide and three or four feet deep. There was only a very narrow log bridge over the stream. It was high too, maybe five feet in the air over the stream. The Fijians crossed with no problem. Their bare feet gave them good traction and grip. But good old' John PC Volunteer slowly ventured out, got to the middle of the log and slipped off into the drink. Splash! Slurp! Through the water and into a foot of mud at the bottom.

I was thoroughly wet and muddy but determined to carry on. The Fijians of course were horrified at what happened to their guest, the "kai vavalagi" (foreigner). But when I came up out of the stream laughing at my own plight, they joined in. We all had a good laugh over my misfortune.

On June 3, 1968, I finally moved from Nawi to Tukavesi and into my own Fijian bure, a thatched bamboo and grass roofed hut about twelve feet wide and eighteen feet long. It was a perfect house both in size and comfort. It had doors on two sides and windows with wood shutters on the other two sides. Cool and airy, it was to be a home base for me. My long itinerant vigil was over. It was a long wait, almost four months to the day after arriving on Vanua Levu in February. I finally had a permanent location, a place of my own.

The house was located on the grounds of the Buca Bay Agriculture Station. The Field Officer for Buca Bay was Savenaca Koroinivalu, a middle-aged career civil servant. His family included his wife, Marama, and their five children, four boys and a girl, ranging in age from 7 to 13. The boys were Savenaca junior, Jone, Bola, Peni and daughter, Naomi. Save and Marama had three older children as well, a married daughter on Viti Levu and two sons away at school on Viti Levu. I would meet the two sons later when they came home to visit.

The journal for June 4, 1968, strongly indicates the presence of children:

"...Speaking of being bugged, Save's kids here are like ants. Just all over the place. They are beautiful little kids though. I just hope they don't get in my hair too much."

Even though by this time my language ability had grown considerably, I was still far from being a totally competent speaker of Fijian.

This fact was not realized by many Fijians, as they would speak rapidly to me and lose me in the process.

No one exemplified this more that did nine-year-old John, or Jone, the family's rascal. John would often come running up to my bure with a machine gun staccato of tongue twisting language. Hopelessly confused and not understanding a word he usually said, I did my best to calm him down and to get him to speak in slower more even tones. Throughout my year and a half of living with the Koroinivalu family, John, my namesake, was always a rascal, especially when it came to talking and telling a story.

My new location at Tukavesi made the work prospects on the census much easier. For one thing, Tukavesi was the government center for all Buca Bay with the school, medical clinic, agriculture, and public works stations all located there. Transportation and communication were centrally located and for our task, this made things much easier.

In early July, the first opportunity to visit Kioa Island to work on the census came up. Kioa was owned by the Ellice Island people who bought the island after World War II. Their home in the Ellice group (north of Fiji) was over-populated and they needed a new location. Thus, they acquired Kioa.

The Kioans are Polynesian and have a distinctly Polynesian culture compared to Melanesian Fiji. But even though they have kept their traditional Ellice culture strong, they have accommodated elements of Fijian culture into their own.

The Kioans can drink yaqona with the best of the Fijians. They enjoy the opportunity to join in on a grog session. Also, many have become bilingual, mastering Fijian as a matter of necessity to get along with the Fijians in the Buca Bay area. Many also speak English as well.

It was this fact of bilingualism that gave me a most amusing incident on that first working visit to Kioa. By July, I was becoming competent in spoken Fijian. This was a necessity for my work of course.

One of the first Kioans I visited received me warmly. After explaining in broken English, interspersed with some sign language, we proceeded to walk out to his food gardens and his coconut groves.

While trying to gain information from him on his land holding, it became obvious that we were not communicating well. He could not really understand English and I could not understand the Ellice dialect. What to do I wondered? I needed to get some pretty accurate information to complete the data for his holding.

Through trial and error, we both finally discovered that each of us could speak good Fijian. Here was the obvious answer!

So, here we were, an English-speaking American and an Ellice speaking Kioan carrying on a happy conversation in Fijian! You might say that we hit upon a multi-cultural solution to an international relations problem. The United Nations would have been pleased.

In fact, that story lent itself well to future grog and talanoa (story) sessions. I got plenty of mileage out of that one. The Fijians loved it when I told the one about the American (me) and the Kioan speaking Fijian on Kioa Island.

From the Amusing Incident Department also comes this little anecdote. I was waiting at Tukavesi to go over to Rabi Island, located in northern Buca Bay. The journal is dated July 29, 1968:

"…Would you believe it? I heard the song 'Silver Bells' by the McGuire Sisters on Radio Fiji this morning. Holy cow! A Christmas song in July in the Fiji Islands! What next I wonder?"

But that was typical of the unexpected events and incidents that made living in Fiji a real adventure. Because everyday life was so humdrum and routine, great value or interest was places on often commonplace or trivial things. Things like a Christmas song in July were big events.

In mid-August I had a chance to return to Kioa for a quick visit to take part in a festival of sorts. A young fellow named Kailopa, son of our agriculture field man there, came to fetch me. The journal entry for August 14, 1968, notes:

"…Kailopa came today and we rode across to Kioa in a canoe. Talk about the Peace Corps experience. Man! Riding across Buca Bay in an outrigger canoe. Can't get more islandish than that. It was really fun though."

The Kioans had invited me to come to Kioa to see some of their native dancing and hear some Ellice singing. It was a real honor to be invited to take part in their celebrations. The journal entry for August 14th continues:

"When you stop to think about it, you know that you are seeing things here and experiencing things that not many people ever dream of seeing back home. How many people have ever seen a real Polynesian dance, like I have seen on Rabi and here on Kioa? Also, many people pay a lot of money to see things like this while its cost me practically nothing. So, I'm really quite fortunate I think to be able to see these things as they actually are."

Again, the fact that in our respective jobs we were able to travel widely throughout the province allowed us to meet a wide variety of people which in turn led us to many different experiences. This was a great benefit from our work.

One of the most enjoyable trips any of us experienced in Cakaudrove was the October 1968, boat trip to Yacata Island. For this special trip, Dave, Charlie, and I teamed up. We were to complete the visit and enumerate a small number of holdings in as short a time as possible. For this reason, all three of us could go, along with one of our census field men. We decided to take Dave's man in Savusavu, Pita Ralaca, one of the more reliable workers.

We left for Yacata on September 30, 1968. Yacata is a small coral island located some thirty miles east of Taveuni. We were to go by boat from Buca Bay via the north point of Taveuni into the open sea. The following entries from the journal cover that trip to Yacata Island.

September 30, 1968:

"Seasick. That is the only way to describe today after a horrible trip from Buca Bay past Taveuni and on to Yacata Island. Oh God! Did I puke on that boat. Man! I really had it. The seas were rough coming over and we had a small boat to make things worse. Anyway, after seeing a big ocean liner, surviving my bouts of hanging over the side, we finally arrived at the beautiful island of Yacata. We were warmly received by the people of Yacata, presented our sevu sevu and had a bit of yaqona tonight."

October 1, 1968:

"…A beautiful day here in Paradise and I think Yacata is really Paradise in Fiji. We did our work today, completing everything. The people here are cooperative and full of fun. After our work today we knew we were in for a real enjoyable evening. The three of us also gave a little talk to the school kids today. It was very well received and was of course in Fijian.

We started the evening with a great feast: fish, chicken, plenty of good Fijian food. Afterwards we were entertained by a great grog session with the girls doing a meke (dance). It was beautiful. The people have gone out of their way to be friendly and kind. We were given many gifts of yaqona, plus the feast, and some coconut oil. All of these were presented in the traditional Fijian ceremonial style. All I can say is that I have been really impressed by the great people of Yacata Island."

October 2, 1968:

"...After saying 'sa moce' (farewell) to the people and snapping many pictures we got on the boat, Dau ni Vatu, to return to Vanua Levu. At the moment we are hung up in the bay, waiting for the tide to come in. It is too shallow to go over the surrounding reef. This island is beautiful this a.m., white sand beaches, palms, breeze, the real South Pacific Paradise man! And there are those cute little girls back in the village— really cute little girls.

The memories of our stay on Yacata are pleasant. We also have a few souvenirs, bottles of coconut oil, shell necklaces or 'salusalus' and just the kindness that was ever present during our stay there."

The Yacata trip was one of the highlights of our entire census work. There were so many good positive things that we gained from the experience. The fact of being royally received and treated by an isolated small island community was just part of it.

But Yacata did not get many visitors and so in a way it was a treat for the island folks too, to have someone from the outside world. Our visit provided them the opportunity to "talanoa" (talk story) with others and learn news of the outside world. Especially when it turned out to be three young Americans working for the Fiji government, well, it called for something special. The people of Yacata responded with an outpouring of welcome and warmth that touched our hearts.

One of Dave's letters to his family touched upon this point. The letter is dated October 4, 1968:

"...The population of Yacata is 270. We measured only eight farms there. The main point is the tremendous generosity we received from the people. They gave us tremendous food, all the fresh fish we could eat, tavioka, buns, butter, and once, even chicken."

One interesting thing I recall specifically was the freshwater situation on Yacata. Since it was a low coral atoll, much of their water supply depended upon rainfall. They had a catchment system of tanks that collected rain runoff from rooftops. For bathing purposes, we were led into the coconut grove on the edge of the village where there was a well of sorts.

It was a hole in the ground, maybe a few feet deep. Here the ground water seeped through the coral sand and was scooped up by the bucket full. So, under a typically gorgeous moonlit Pacific sky, there we were squatting in a coconut grove splashing water over ourselves and taking a bath in a bucket. It was truly a Micheneresque (he the author of <u>Tales of the South Pacific)</u> experience.

With our work completed in one day's time, we gathered our gear and departed on the third day. We left Yacata with hearts full of warmth and gratitude to the beautiful people who call it their home. It was one of the most gratifying experiences of our entire stay in Fiji.

We returned to Tukavesi and my base to await another boat to take us to Qelelevu Island, a small coral atoll to the far north of Vanua Levu. Our wait for Qelelevu was a time for reflection. The spell of the Pacific was upon us as evident from my journal of October 6, 1968:

"...Tonight, we just took a walk up the road to the point where you can see Tukavesi, Buca Bay, Kioa and Taveuni. It was peaceful up there tonight. It really set you in the mood of the South Pacific to just stand there and take it all in."

That mood of the South Pacific was often a stupefying, mind dulling acceptance of routine. Plain and simple routine. It permeated your life, your habits, and your attitudes. It was magnified when you realized that you were on a small island in a large ocean. You were in a remote isolated area far removed from any vestiges of civilization as you know it.

It had a way of coming back at you and reminding you of the fact. The realization struck when we waited for our boat to Qelelevu Island. The journal entries describe it aptly.

October 8, 1968:

"...Well, after rising early and making it over to Nutuvu, we spent the whole day waiting for the boat to Qelelevu, which didn't come."

October 9, 1968:

"...Well, we're still waiting for the boat. Guess we will not go today. Nobody seems to know what is going on about the boat. What is more, nobody seems to care whether we go or not. Funny how things can get so mixed up and confused in this country."

Nevertheless, after several days of waiting, the government boat, Cagi-mai-ra (Westwind), arrived in Buca Bay on October 10th and we were soon on our way to Qelelevu. It would be the second outer island trip that Dave, Charlie, and I would take together for the agriculture census. In the wake of Yacata, the visit to Qelelevu was somewhat anti-climatic.

The journal for October 11, 1968, notes:

"Arrived at Qelelevu around noon. Really a pretty small island; flat, rocky, with plenty of coconuts. A huge reef, some 12 miles long

follows up to the island in a sort of semi-circle. We went ashore, presented our yaqona and went to work. Man! What a place. Those people
grow their food on nothing but old reef patches. But everything grows
well despite it. We finished our work by 5:00pm and returned to the
boat. Wanted to stay but we had to get the boat off the reef before the
tide went down."

One little note of interest about Qelelevu concerns the lousy mosquitoes there. The atoll had a plague of mosquitoes that caused sheer
misery. That was another reason for our fast work and quick getaway
on the boat. Frankly, we did not want to spend too much time there.

The contrasting lifestyles that we had seen during those two
weeks made many impressions upon us. While the people of Vanua
Levu, where we were based, lived basically the same as the Yacata and
Qelelevu people there were differences. Perhaps the biggest difference
was the fact of isolation on a small coral atoll compared to living on a
larger high island. The sense of isolation was not so great on a larger
island and one felt more at ease with the general state of things.

The journal entry for October 13 notes:

"…As I look back on our trips this past two weeks, I feel that I've
really seen a lot of Fiji. The differences between the ways of life of the
people on Vanua Levu, Yacata and Qelelevu are great. It's really been
a great opportunity to see these different places. I know that many impressions of the people and things I've seen haven't come to me yet. It's
hard to put them down on paper. But I know that I will always remember the things I have seen out there."

Progress on the agriculture census in October 1968, was picking up
considerably over the first few months. However, we were still behind
schedule on many fronts throughout the province.

It was at this point that our boss, Agriculture Officer for Cakaudrove Province, Josua Cavalevu, decided some drastic action was needed to remedy the Taveuni problem. Inasmuch as I had my hands full supervising the Buca Bay area and doing some of the actual field work also, Josua transferred supervision of Taveuni to one of the regular staff members on Taveuni.

I remember being somewhat upset about this action, mainly from the fact that I was not even consulted prior to the action being taken. I found out about it after the fact.

The transfer of supervisory responsibilities left my pride a little bruised at first, but it turned out to be a blessing in disguise. Taveuni needed closer attention that what I could give it and the field officer there who took control of the census completed it successfully. It all turned out for the better in the end.

Being relieved of the responsibility for Taveuni, I could now focus complete attention on Buca Bay, and the three of us together could coordinate our efforts on the remaining months of the census on mainland Cakaudrove.

In the period from November through December 1968, we were being pressured to pick up the pace of progress on the agriculture census. The target date for completion of February 1, 1969, was rapidly approaching. Our boss, Josua Cavalevu, was continually checking our progress. We were still battling the problems of transportation and communication, especially with our field men. Progress toward completion was being made, especially in comparison to the early months of the project. With several months experience behind us, we three Volunteers were also coming into our own. We were familiar with our work, we were now able to find our way around in the bush, in the villages, and with the people. We were rapidly learning the language. Simply, we were learning survival in the bush.

By mid-December 1968, I had the census nearing completion in my own area of northern Buca Bay. Because of this, I agreed to accompany Charlie up Natewa Bay to his area for a few days to assist. I could afford to spend a couple of working days away from Buca Bay.

We travelled by boat from lower Natewa Bay north to Korotasere, Charlie's home base, and spent the night of December 16, 1968, there. The next day we began a hike down the coast south (from where we had come the previous day), toward the Hibiscus Highway, some 20 miles away. Our first stop was the village of Koronatonga, about eight miles below Korotasere. We walked the distance in a light misting rain and followed coastal trails most of the way.

At times, we cut inland, up, and over bush hill trails that some-what shortened our hike. It was incredibly hot and muggy climbing up those hills. Sweat poured from every part of your body and your clothes would stick to your skin. Only upon reaching the summit of a hill could you breathe a sigh of relief for there would usually be a cool breeze coming in from the ocean to give some comfort. The usually panoramic vista of the green hills and blue lagoons of Natewa Bay also added to the relief one experienced.

We made it to Koronatonga and saw the farmers Charlie had on his list. After overnighting in the village on December 17th, we again started out down the coast with Wainigata Cocoa Station as our goal for that night. Wainigata was the agriculture station located at the end of the road near lower Natewa Bay, near the Hibiscus Highway running up from Savusavu.

We visited a couple of Indian farmers on the way down the next day, measured their holding, and moved on through a couple of more villages on down the coast.

An interesting journal entry regarding these villages is on December 18, 1968:

"...An interesting thing about Fijian customs; as we walked through one village this afternoon, several houses were just eating their midday meal. We were invited by several people to 'Lako mai, kana!' (come and eat). Even though we were 'strangers' in the village we were invited to rest, eat, and relax. This is one of the beautiful things about Fijian customs and culture. Things like this really set apart this society from that in the States or any other western country."

On the last stretch of our hike that day we came to a rain swollen river in a cattle pasture. The river was perhaps 30-feet wide and turned out to be chest deep. Charlie and I were both somewhat exhausted from the day's hike of several miles already and did not particularly like having to wade a river.

We could find no log crossing in the area. So, we finally decided to wade the river. Not wanting to completely soak our clothes we stripped naked except for our rugged jungle boots. That done, we hoisted our packs over our heads and begun wading that river. I remember thinking at the time that it would be terrible to have an aggressive fish or something else inhabiting that river to come and check out our exposed private parts!

Making it safely, but with due apprehension, to the other side of the river, we headed for the nearest tree to quickly put our clothes back on. At that time too, considering our rather embarrassing situation, and being a fairly exposed open pasture area, Charlie couldn't help remarking to me, "Wow, John, if somebody saw us out here prancing around in our birthday suits, they would sure begin to wonder about us!"

I answered, "Charlie, if anybody shows up, I'll just pretend that I don't know you!"

Charlie always had a remarkable sense of humor and a very quick wit. He prided himself on it.

We made it finally to Wainigata for the night. Never were we so glad to arrive at a station. Both of us were hungry, exhausted, and damp from the rain-soaked hike we had made down from Korotasere. The rainy season was upon us at that time and it was something that would add another discomfiting dimension to our outdoor work on the census.

The journal for December 19, 1968, notes:

"...More rain today. Seems like the rainy season is really coming in now. All this week while I was in Natewa Bay I was hardly able to stay dry. Most of my clothes are wet and smell rank. After living out of the same pack and clothes for almost two weeks everything just turns bad after a while. That's one thing about our jobs here. We spend a lot of time living out of packs and living away from our 'homes.' I have hardly seen Tukavesi in two weeks."

For us to take part in the festivities of our first Fijian Christmas and New Year's celebrations, work on the census was suspended for the few days prior to and during the holidays.

The pace however, picked up again right after New Year's Day, 1969. Perhaps in fact, things started out in the New Year with a bad omen for me. On the very last day of 1968, on returning from a staff meeting in Savusavu, my briefcase containing my wallet, journal, working papers, and so on, was accidently misplaced with the Taveuni Island staff. All my important papers ended up on Taveuni. Because the Taveuni agriculture staff had returned via Land Rover with us to Buca Bay and then to Taveuni by boat, my case was put off with their gear. I did not notice it until it was too late.

For over two weeks, I was completely without my journal and other working papers, including my checkbook! I recall having a small amount of money in my pockets and perhaps some in my bure at Tukavesi. Somehow, I must have gotten by during that time. Of course, one can live for practically nothing in a Fijian village when it comes right down to it.

It was during this two-week period just after New Year's Day, 1969 that I had an occasion to head off into the bush once again with Charlie. This time it was on Natewa Bay again only on the eastern side, the Tunuloa District which bordered my area of Buca Bay.

Charlie's field man for that area, Esala Cagi, accompanied us on the weeklong operation into the bush. The main reason we concentrated in this area was because progress was slow, and our February census completion date was rapidly approaching. We needed to coordinate our efforts throughout the province if we were to successfully complete this project on time. So, here we were once again, charging off headlong into a week's excursion I called the Tunuloa Caper. Mostly for our own amusement, we gave our various treks, missions, and operations out in the bush special names, sort of like the military calls its special operations by unique names.

I cannot even recall the exact dates, other than it took place during the period January 1-15, 1969. It began with the Land Rover dropping Charlie, Esala and myself, off in mid-afternoon at the village of Koroinivonu in north Buca Bay. We immediately struck out through the bush heading west, up and over the hills and through the jungle. The trail was a good one, clearly marked and easy to follow. However, it was somewhat hazardous with many large tree roots exposed on the ground. This made it easy to trip and stumble. Rain compounded the problem by making the path muddy and slippery.

And rain indeed it did. We had started out the hike in good weather, but by the time we had climbed several hundred feet through the bush hills, the clouds opened and drenched us thoroughly. We quickened our pace to gain the summit and then descend to a dryer side over and beyond the hills to the west. At times, we were running full tilt which made it even more hazardous due to the slippery path and large tree roots on the ground.

Esala, the tough Fijian that he was, led the way on our over-the-hill venture. He was quite far ahead of Charlie and me when we finally reached the summit and got out from under the torrential downpour. Exhausted from our trek through the bush and now feeling the heat and mugginess of the day we began our descent down the hills leading to the eastern coast of Natewa Bay. We soon passed a farmer's garden plot located at a high elevation up in the hills. Right on the pathway stood a large pineapple plant with a small pineapple on it.

Both of us, tired and needing a rest and with an enormous thirst, stopped dead in our tracks.

"Charlie," I said eyeing that pineapple, "let's eat that pineapple!"

Nodding in agreement, Charlie needed no further encouragement. "Let's do it!" he said.

I whipped out a pocketknife and we were soon refreshing ourselves with an unknown farmer's pineapple. Nothing ever tasted better.

After our short break, Charlie and I continued our descent and soon caught up with Esala down on the coast. Here we picked up a new trail to the village of Salia, our goal for the day. Teasingly, Esala asked us, "Hey, where have you two been?"

Charlie replied sheepishly, "Oh, we had to take a short rest and eat a pineapple."

Esala laughed, "I thought that's what you were doing. I saw that small pineapple along the path and figured you two would stop to eat it!"

We all had a good laugh over the incident of the stolen pineapple.

The jungle trail we had followed, up and over the hills and down to the coast was probably only six miles long. But it had been a tough exhausting hike, nonetheless. We were happy to arrive at Salia which was only a mile or so down the coast from where our overland trail ended. Tired, wet, and hungry, we were taken into the "turaga-ni-koro's" (village chief's) house and were soon served steaming hot cups of tea. For our parched throats, it was soothing relief and we each had several cups.

With our clothes drenched and even what we had in our packs damp; we needed a solution to dry our clothes. It did not look like the weather would cooperate much, so we hit upon a novel solution: the copra dryer. We took our clothes and hung them over the village copra dryer. In a short time, our clothes were nice and dry but with a slight problem: they smelled like old copra gunny sacks with a nice aromatic coconut fragrance. But with the tropical downpours we had during that week, we never forgot our unique solution for wet clothes: the copra dryer.

It was during this trip to Salia that I remember an amusing incident with Charlie. Because we did live out of packs for days at a time and had little chance to wash our clothes, that fact soon became very noticeable. Copra dryer clothes did not help much either. I was following Charlie a few yards back as we trekked through the bush one afternoon and kept noticing a strong odor, one suggesting sweaty moldy clothes and moldy copra bags.

I suggested nonchalantly to Charlie, "Hey, Charlie, I think you need a change of clothes. I can smell you a mile away!"

Charlie, not to be outdone, countered by saying, "Hey, you better take a good whiff of yourself. You aren't in any better shape than me!"

And he was right. After too many days out in the bush, it was difficult to stay clean or to even have clean clothes. The high humidity and drenching rains made our lives somewhat uncomfortable in the bush.

The week in eastern Natewa Bay was a difficult one. After completing the census work in Salia, we were undecided as to how we would get out of there and back to our stations. Again, transportation was a problem. We had none. The only thing we could do was walk out. None of us were game enough to go overland the way we came in and it was a longer distance of some 20 miles down to the lower end of Natewa Bay where we could get to the Hibiscus Highway.

Charlie knew the medical officer, the Fijian doctor, in this area. He suggested that we hike to that station and see if there would not be a boat that could take us to lower Natewa Bay. So, off we went, a hike of some six or eight miles along the coast to near the village of Drekeniwai, where the doctor had his bush clinic.

After practically an all-day hike, we arrived tired and exhausted as usual. The doctor graciously welcomed us to his comfortable western-style government-built house. It was the typical cement block tin-roofed house the government provides its civil servants in most locations.

We arrived on a Saturday and discovered that there was no boat to take us to Matakunia on lower Natewa Bay. However, we did learn that a boat was due in on Sunday. It would be transporting some medical officials back up the coast of Natewa Bay from where we had just come. The boat could probably drop us off at or near Napuka Mission, which was around the point to the north of where we were now and at the top of Buca Bay.

Well, we thought, it is not exactly the way we wanted to go, but then things never do turn out the way you want them to when you are out in the bush. We laid over at the doctor's house and managed to at least wash our clothes. If nothing else, that was an achievement. It was certainly something that needed doing.

We managed to catch the boat the next day. It took us back to the north point of Tunuloa peninsula where we landed at the village of Nailou. Here we stayed for the night and the next day found our way around to Napuka Mission, a walk of only two or three miles. From there, we caught a ride on the Buca Bay bus bound for Savusavu. The bus originated in Napuka at the end of the road.

The Tunuloa Caper finally came to an end and we managed to get out of the bush. It was the end of a particularly difficult week in the bush of eastern Natewa Bay. The journal entry for January 1969, describes it as such:

January 1-15, 1969:

"...and spending a whole week out in the bush over on Natewa Bay, Tunuloa side. It was a time when I felt like I might lose my mind from being caught out in the bush, the new villages I saw, the people, walking through the bush, up hills and down, the beaches. How many miles did we walk? Charlie, I, and Esala the field man, walking maybe 30-40 miles in that week.

And the rain, coming down in buckets. Finally making it back to Tukavesi. Down to Savusavu again; within eight days time, sleeping in five different places; constantly on the move. Sometimes at Salia, getting little sleep due to grog and dancing every night. But the sweet, sweet memories of it, even though it was physically exhausting."

The agriculture census, an incredibly difficult, tiring, and exhausting undertaking, was still not quite complete, but it was getting there. There were only a few more holders in the entire province to measure and then we would be done, right on the February 1ˢᵗ target date.

CHAPTER 9

OPERATION PLAY IT COOL

Come the end of January 1969, the agriculture census for Cakaudrove Province was completed. All the farmers and land holders in the entire province that were on our lists were visited and the land, animals, and crops were measured and counted. Some 1200 farms and land holdings had been included. The seemingly insurmountable task had been accomplished. At least we thought we were finished.

Dave, Charlie, and I had been looking forward to completing our work on the census and then taking a much-needed two-week leave to Suva. We had been up in the bush country for five months, since late August 1968, our first real leave time. We were ready for a change of scene. We were quite psyched up for a vacation in the city and away from the hardships of the bush. Our spirits soared as we contemplated our upcoming leave. Our morale was boosted considerably by the prospects over the waning days of January.

And now, with the census completed by the February 1st. target date, we could unload the pressures that had been building for months.

And then suddenly, our leaves were wiped out, the wind taken out of our sails, our spirits and morale totally dashed.

To our horror and consternation, the central census office in Suva wanted the entire Wailevu West district redone. And what is more, it was to be redone right away before we went on leave. They extended the completion date until February 20th.

The problem came about during the early months of the census in 1968. One of the census field men working under Dave's supervision was caught falsifying some census report forms. The man in fact was filling in the census forms without even having visited the farms concerned. Dave discovered the errors when he cross-checked some of the supposedly measured holdings. The man eventually confessed to the cover up and was terminated from the census work.

So now, at the end of the census period of one calendar year, we were ordered to return to the field and remeasure all the holdings that the released field man had turned in as completed. The census office demanded accuracy and it was decided not to trust the earlier reports on the chance that they too had been falsified.

And so here we were, the three of us Volunteers, so long up in the bush of Cakaudrove with our leave to Suva suddenly taken away from us. We were physically and mentally exhausted from so many weeks and months in the bush and constantly being on the move. To us, this was a spiritually crushing blow to our morale. We were distraught and asked if we could complete the job after our scheduled leaves. No, that was not possible we were told. It was necessary to complete the census now.

Sullen, dejected and with spirits sagging extremely low, we searched for something to console us. How could they do this to us? We pondered that question repeatedly but could find no easy answer. It was the simple fact that after all the hard work, the difficult circumstances, and the exhausting efforts we had put forth on the census, we were being asked to summon up one last great push to complete the job.

The task that we now faced was even more difficult than the one we faced back in February 1968, when we first began our work. With a year's experience in the bush we now knew how arduous our task would be. We needed something or someone who would help us to summon up the courage and strength to face the task ahead. We found our solace, our hero, in Cool Hand Luke.

Charlie, Dave and I had recently read the book, Cool Hand Luke, the story of a petty criminal in the southern United States who becomes a hero to his fellow jail inmates by continually bucking the establishment with his exploits and daring escapes. Cool Hand Luke made it a habit to "play it cool" despite difficult circumstances. Because Luke kept his cool, he became a hero to those around him. Because of the similar adversity that we faced in our final push on the census, Luke became our "hero" and inspiration.

We were determined to "play it cool" and not let this Wailevu thing get us down. We wanted to just "get on up there boss!" as Luke often said. For these reasons, we code named our final Wailevu offensive on the census "Operation Play It Cool." With typical stiff-lipped British perseverance and our own brand of bush humor, we faced our final and toughest assignment yet.

Within the given three-week extension period until February 20, 1968, the census office wanted us to complete as many land holdings in Wailevu as possible. Recognizing the difficulty of the task we faced, they compromised their original request that all Wailevu be redone and agreed to accept as many as we could redo in three weeks. This made the situation a little more tolerable for us. Nevertheless, we formed a team of five or six of our field men plus the three of us and set out on February 4th for Wailevu.

Wailevu district of Cakaudrove Province is located southwest from Savusavu across Savusavu Bay. The district makes up the lower portion of Cakaudrove Province and borders on the extreme southern peninsula and province of Bua. Wailevu is a very remote isolated district, reached only by boat or by walking around the coast of Savusavu Bay. There are no roads, towns, or modern communications in the Wailevu district.

We took the shortest and most direct route to Wailevu, straight across the bay some 12-15 miles. The journal for Tuesday, February 4, 1969, describes it as such:

"...Off to Wailevu today with almost the entire Cakaudrove census team along. Had lunch on a sand dune on a reef then pushed farther on by boat. Dave and Charlie got off a few miles up and I now find myself in an isolated village in Wailevu named Naigagi. Will push on farther up the river here tomorrow to visit other villages. This is a rather bush koro (village) as we had to follow up a river a few miles before arriving. I am with two of the field men who will assist me in my work. Tomorrow I will try to join up with Dave and Charlie."

To cover as much territory as possible, we divided our team into two- and three-man squads. We felt that the work would go much faster and nobody would feel alone out in the unfamiliar area of Wailevu. Remembering that the fellows who worked with us had been working alone in other areas of the province during the year, we felt it would be beneficial to have them work together in this final push of the census. Also, as supervisors, we could see that the expense of effort these fellows had been making for the past year was also beginning to show on them. We felt that a coordination of efforts was needed on this final phase of the census.

Over the next couple of days, I worked my way up the coast through a couple of villages, seeing farmers along the way. We were entertained by the villagers each night, usually drinking plenty of grog and watching the women perform "mekes" (dances) for us.

I arrived in the village of Nutuvu (not the same place as the Nutuvu in Buca Bay) and met up with Dave and Charlie. Leaving our squads in the bush, the three of us caught the boat back to Savusavu on Thursday, February 6th. We were scheduled for a meeting in Savusavu with the census officer from Suva to discuss the Wailevu situation.

As we left the village of Nutuvu where Dave and Charlie had spent the previous night, they told me of an unusual experience. They told me that I had arrived one day late. When I asked why, they said that for supper the night before they had been served horse meat. It was the first time that either of them had ever eaten horse in a Fijian village. I had never had it myself. Normally Fijians do not eat horse meat but apparently this village did. Maybe they were having hard times and had already eaten all their cattle and pigs.

Since it was the end of the week, we did not return to Wailevu. The boat returned to Wailevu and brought back our field men for the weekend in Savusavu. We had a brief respite in Savusavu by enjoying a meal or two at Ping Ho's Café, our usual hangout in town and even took in a movie at the theater.

The journal notes that weekend, Sunday, February 9, 1969:

"...went to town for the afternoon movie, 'The Savage,' an Indian-U.S. Calvary movie about the Sioux Indians starring Charleton Heston, made in 1952! It was good for kicks anyway. Back to Dave's tonight to plan the week's work in Wailevu."

At the beginning of the second week of Operation Play It Cool, I found myself deep in the Wailevu district again at the village of Nakasa. The village was perhaps an extraordinary one as villages go. It was clean and well kept, had lots of pretty flowers and hedge bushes throughout the village green. It also had an incredibly good water supply and something I never came across before in any other Fijian village: flush toilets! As far as I knew, it was the only village in all Cakaudrove to have such modern facilities. To find something like this in the heart of bush country, well, it just seemed incredible.

I had one of the field men with me on this part of the operation, Esala, the man who also accompanied Charlie and me on the Tunuloa Caper. We spent two days at Nakasa looking up some of the farmers in the area and remeasuring their land holdings. Overall, Nakasa was a very pleasant place in which to work, despite its relative isolated and remote location. We were treated very well by the people, had good food and facilities, and did not stay up too late at night drinking grog or dancing.

The third day, February 12th, we struck out for Wailevu village, the center of the Wailevu district. It was located a few miles up the coast from Nakasa. As I recall, Esala and I visited a few farmers on our way up to Wailevu. We were to rendezvous with Dave, Charlie, and the rest of the team there.

Having spent the night in Wailevu, the entire team now concentrated on villages in and around the immediate area. Wailevu village sits at the mouth of a small river that empties into Savusavu Bay. We followed this river up into the interior of the island a few miles, visiting several new villages. It was a terrifically difficult hike as the hills were quite rugged and the trails were wet and muddy.

The journal entry for February 13, 1969, notes:

"...A very hard field day. Walked a good eight miles and visited four new villages, way up in the interior of Wailevu district. Returned to the village of Wailevu tonight. Was really exhausted."

It is difficult to describe the experience of tramping around in the bush and jungle all day long measuring and counting a farmer's land holdings. Most of the time, a man would have a specific area of coconuts that he utilized, or that belonged to his "mataqali," or clan. But as for his "tei teis," his food gardens, well, these could number several and could be scattered locations. Since it was necessary to measure the dimensions of each food plot and draw a diagram of it on the census report form, we had to tramp around the bush hills to see each one. It made for a tiring job. Most farmers had more than one garden and many had several.

On Friday, February 14th, we returned to Savusavu by boat for the weekend. We were quite pleased so far with the results of our final operation. The team working together was proving efficient and completing a good number of holdings. Our coordinated efforts were paying off. What is more, the spirit and morale of our team were still high. Working together was invaluable.

The weekend was spent completing the census report forms for the holdings done that week. It was also a time to just rest and relax. The two weeks had been hard, but we were now down to our last week in the bush.

Our third and last week of "Operation Play It Cool" started out on a bad note. On Monday, February 17th, the boat's outboard engine would not start. The agriculture department's boat driver and mechanic, a part-Chinese and part-Fijian man named Wing Ting, could not get the thing started. We waited all morning and most of the afternoon but to no avail.

So, there we sat in Savusavu. Perhaps it was better than being down in the Wailevu bush country. We did utilize our time that day by writing a first draft of our final census report for Cakaudrove Province. We again spent the night, as we had the past couple of weekends, at Dave's place, just outside of town.

The next day, Tuesday, February 18th, found the boat's engine once again in good running order. The team gathered up its gear and headed off for the last assault of "Operation Play It Cool." This would be the final phase for us. By the end of the week, the census for Cakaudrove would be done.

The journal entry for February 18th. describes the beginning of the last week in Wailevu:

"Tonight, I find myself in Dawara village, a far down as you can go in Cakaudrove Province since it is near the border of Bua Province. It was hot on the boat coming down and I got good sunburn. I feel very tired this evening, must be from the sun's heat. I was accompanied by three field men and have only two days to work before we go back to Savusavu. So, it's not all bad. Am certainly glad we don't have too long to go before we finish."

Being way down in southern Wailevu, the southernmost point in Cakaudrove, was somewhat of an achievement for me. I had been to the far points of Buca Bay peninsula as well as Taveuni Island. With this trip, I had covered a good deal of the province, all except for the Sagani area that was Charlie's territory. That area extends all the way to the far northern tip of the island of Vanua Levu.

But to be able to say that I've been to Dawara is to say a lot. On the other hand, it is not much really. It is just another bush village, remote, isolated, a backwater of a remote isolated province. At any rate, my field man and I spent a couple of days in the area, visiting and trying to locate as many farmers as we could by February 20th.

On the 20th, we took the boat on a slow ride up to Wailevu village once again, where we were to meet Dave and Charlie and the rest of the team. We arrived by mid-day, had our lunch, and took off for Savusavu across the bay. All in all, "Operation Play It Cool" was a brutal, punishing, demanding three weeks. It did however bring out the best in us and in our team of field men. With their help and cooperation, we were able to complete a good deal of the Wailevu district for the census.

One thing that I recall as we rode the boat back to Savusavu that afternoon of February 20th. was the feeling of relief to have the job done.

We were not ecstatic; I think we were all too tired to be that excited. Generally, we were just all glad to finally have the job over and done with. We knew that at least we would not have to go back out into the bush and villages for the sake of measuring and plotting out somebody's garden plots. It was a tremendous relief to be free of it all.

One amusing incident that I do recall in the waning days of the trip was a big crab roast we had. One afternoon Charlie and I arrived at the meeting place on the beach near a copra dryer. We found all the fellows munching on a huge beautiful crab they had caught on the reef. They had thrown it on the fire of the dryer and were now enjoying fresh baked crab. Charlie and I eagerly dug in and it was a terrific afternoon treat as we sat on a beautiful South Pacific sandy beach with the blue bay and lagoon stretching out before us.

We spent Friday, February 21st, at the office in Savusavu completing the final census forms and aerial photographs for Wailevu. We prepared everything for turning into the census office when we went to Suva. We had also requested that our field men remain in Savusavu on Friday night as we planned a party for them to celebrate the official end of the agriculture census for Cakaudrove Province.

Dave, Charlie and I supplied the food from Ping Ho's Café and all the beer for our entire census team. To say the least, we had a rousing good time with the fellows. I believe that they sincerely appreciated the party we threw for them. We expressed our sincerest thanks for all their efforts, hard work, and diligence over the past year. We had grown to know these men very well and it would now be hard to say farewell to them. But we had profited, individually and collectively, from knowing each of them. The census could not have been completed without their assistance.

In true Fijian fashion, we all got good and drunk at our party. We shared some of the experiences and things that had happened to us during the census work over the past year. After we had eaten and drunk more beer, some of the fellows wanted to go drink yaqona in the village. We were invited but politely declined.

There was a movie on at the theater in Savusavu that night and so Dave, Charlie, and I took our leave from the fellows and began walking the short distance to town and the theater. Typically, as Fijian village boys would, we locked arms around shoulders and staggered down the road singing Fijian songs. We were totally drunk and happy to be all done with the census work. We were letting it all hang out.

We arrived at the theater in a somewhat boisterous and frivolous state and no doubt caused a commotion as we stumbled into the theater and found some seats. I don't even recall the film we saw, but it was no doubt one of those cheap "B" movies from the 40's or 50's that were filled with rip-roaring action and sordid romance so popular with the Fijians.

The one thing that I do recall is a Fijian coming up to us on the road after the movie and saying to us, "Hey, you guys acted just like us!" And there we were, unashamedly drunk, loud, and happy, being paid the ultimate compliment by a Fijian. It was another example of the close relationship we had established with the people of Cakaudrove.

And so, Operation Play It Cool drew to a close. It had been a very tough three weeks. It had been a very tough year. Except for clearing up a few administrative details and typing a final report on the census, the three of us were now ready for our long-awaited Suva leaves. We had "played it cool" and successfully completed the census for Cakaudrove.

For Charlie and me, it was time to return to our bases, finish up any work details, gather some fresh clothes together, and just relax for a few days before taking off to Suva.

The journal for Saturday, February 22nd notes:

"...Well, after 19 days away from Tukavesi, I finally made it back today to 'Home Sweet Home.' It felt so great to come back again. It had been so long since I'd left to go to Wailevu."

After a few days rest in Tukavesi, I was to be off to Savusavu once again. Only this time, we weren't headed for the bush of Wailevu. We were headed for the bright lights of Suva. After five months and three weeks of surviving in the bush, the Cakaudrove Team, the "bush apes," were heading for the big city.

CHAPTER 10

GOING ON LEAVE

It is hard to describe the feeling of elation one has in arriving in a big city after being in the bush country for almost six months. For the three of us, few words could describe how we felt. We were just so glad to be out of the country and back into some semblance of civilization as we knew it. This meant a soft bed, hot water showers, decent western food, movies, cars, and all the other conveniences a city has to offer.

Suva of course is small as cities go, perhaps 50,000 population. But for us, used to the small town of Savusavu and the bush villages of Cakaudrove, it was a metropolis. It had all the luxuries and amusements we could ever want. It was definitely a great place to be after the prolonged period we had spent in the bush.

In February 1969, we were ready for a rousing good time in the it. After arriving at Nausori Airport on the 40-minute flight from Savusavu, we rode the bus into Suva, a distance of 10 or 12 miles. We usually checked into one of the reasonable and conveniently located guest houses near the city's center. At the guest houses, one could get bed, shower, and breakfast for about $3.00. It was quite reasonable. It was far better than staying at one of the tourist hotels where rooms were three and four times as much.

One of the first orders of business when we hit town and after finding a place to stay was to find a good pub to have a couple of beers. Once again, we toasted our arrival in Suva and our continuing success at hacking it in the bush. We thoroughly washed away months of accumulated jungle rot with several cold Fiji Beers. This done, we knew for sure that we had arrived in Suva.

It was then on up to the Peace Corps Office, located not far above the center of downtown Suva. Here we checked in and caught up on all the news of our other Volunteer friends. The staff too was always delighted to see us, especially since we came into town so infrequently. The director and assistants were always eager to learn about our work and everything in general about our assignments up on Vanua Levu. And of course, we always had a turn with the Peace Corps doctor who checked us out to make sure we were surviving the rigors of bush living.

It was always great to see some of the other Volunteers, many of whom we knew well in training but had seen little of after arriving in country. It was always great to exchange experiences and to find out how others were coping with their situation. Somehow you always came away from such encounters believing that maybe you were not doing too badly after all.

One instance of meeting a Volunteer whom I had not seen in a long time occurred one afternoon in Suva during this leave. This poor fellow, John Pohlman, had been stationed on a very remote isolated atoll as a teacher. He came to Suva very rarely, even less than we did. At any rate, I met him one afternoon on a street corner in Suva,

I asked him, "Say John, how are you? What are you doing here?"

He answered with a very faraway look in his eyes, "Oh, just watching the cars." And it was a fact. He was just watching the traffic go by.

He was standing there in shorts, T-shirt, and bare footed on a street corner in downtown Suva just watching cars. He had been on his tiny atoll far too long. This was an indication to me that perhaps our situation up in Cakaudrove was not so bad after all.

Sadly, John Pohlman was drafted a few months later and ended up flying helicopters in the Viet Nam war. In a tragic ending, he was killed in action when his helicopter was shot down. John was one of many who gave his all in service for his country.

One of the nicer things about being in Suva was the access to good restaurant food. Compared to first class five-star dining eateries, the small cafes, and places we frequented were probably tacky, but to us they were terrific. When you have gone with practically nothing anyway, almost anything will be a big improvement. As much as we liked Ping Ho's Café in Savusavu, we reveled in the restaurants and cafes of Suva.

It was simply great to get some decent western-style foods such as steak and potatoes, omelets, plenty of fresh vegetables, not to mention sweets like pastries, ice cream and so on. Suva to us was a veritable gourmet's paradise.

We could afford to eat well too, even to indulge in a big tourist hotel meal or two while on leave. Our normal living allowance of $50.00 per months may not have lasted very long on leave and the Peace Corps saw to it that we were granted special leave allowance. This was a bonus to use while on leave and amounted to a few extra dollars per each day of leave taken. This made it even easier to enjoy ourselves while on leave.

Being in Fiji for leave however did present some problems. Where would one go and what would one do? By Peace Corps policy we were not allowed to exit the country during our leave time the first year. We were expected to stay in the country and spend our time learning more about the culture we lived in. This of course pretty much limited where you would go and what you would do when you get there.

The main island of Viti Levu was the most developed, had the most roads, cars, hotels, movies, etc. Parts of it were still isolated and inaccessible, but for the most part it was developed. Vanua Levu, our island, was the second most developed but lagged considerably behind Viti Levu. The other choices were the outer islands in the other districts of the group, mostly small islands, some accessible by air but most reached only by occasional inter-island trading ship.

During our first leave of two weeks in August 1968, Dave, Charlie, and I took advantage of the time to travel around all of Viti Levu. During the several days we had, we spent some time in Suva and then headed west by bus for Sigatoka to visit our friends, James and Nuku Makasiale. James had been transferred to the agriculture department in Sigatoka from his post at Savusavu where we first met him.

We stayed with James and Nuku in their home in Sigatoka for a few days, touring the beautiful Sigatoka Valley, one of Fiji's top agriculture areas, with Big James. We also visited with two good Volunteer buddies, Ron Moore, and Reggie Berry, who worked for the Sigatoka Valley Co-operative. Between Ron and Reggie, and James and Nuku, we were treated to a swinging time of cookouts and parties at the Makasiale home.

From Sigatoka we continued west and north around Viti Levu, through the town of Nadi, where the international airport is located. Then it was on to Lautoka, the second largest town in Fiji. Lautoka is the home of the sugar industry in Fiji, as it is in the heart of Viti Levu's sugar cane country.

We spent a few days in this area and continued around the north and east sides of the island making a complete circle around Viti Levu. All in all, it was a very enjoyable trip and gave us insight into what other parts of Fiji were like.

Because Cakaudrove is almost all virgin bush jungle and coconuts on the low coastal areas, we tended to think that all of Fiji was the same. This trip around Viti Levu changed those misconceptions considerably. We saw that Fiji had contrasting countryside, from jungle to beach, to hot dry sugar cane country, to quite barren dry land in the northwest and north of Viti Levu. I recall being so impressed by northern Viti Levu because it reminded me of South Dakota and Wyoming with wide open spaces and dry hills.

At any rate, during the second year of service, our leave could be extended to outside of Fiji if we so wished. Some Volunteers took advantage of that policy to visit countries nearby like New Zealand, Tonga, Samoa, and others. Dave, Charlie, and I decided that perhaps we would wait until we finished the two years of service before we took out to other countries.

We decided that after being up in the bush of Cakaudrove working on that census it was good enough to be getting out of that place and coming to Suva. Our state of mind in February 1969, was that Suva was a darn good place to be on our leave. We were awfully glad to just be there. We had waited a long time for that.

Other than the renewing of old friendships, enjoying some beer and good food, we were also looking for a good time otherwise. That meant the night life in the city.

Some of our Suva friends came to our aid on these occasions. We generally considered the Volunteers in Suva to be somewhat more sophisticated and dignified than ourselves. After all, we three were just "bush apes" from Cakaudrove. We did not get to the city too often and even when we did, we did not quite know what to do, where to go for fun, or how to act "city like." In a sense, we had become Fijianized to the extent that we forgot how to behave in the city.

Anyway, our Suva friends came through by taking us to parties and night spots where we got to meet many beautiful local girls. Suva was full of beautiful girls. Being somewhat of an ethnic melting pot, many girls carried mixed blood lines. The results were simply lovely.

To three guys coming direct from the bush, a party at someone's place or a night drinking and dancing at a hotel or night club was a real treat. The girls we met through our Suva buddies were also looking for a good time and we generally hit it off well. The fact that we three had come from the wilds of Cakaudrove made us something like celebrities to the local Suva girls. They were amazed by how well we spoke Fijian and how well we knew the people, customs, etc. Compared to the local Suva Volunteers they knew, the girls thought we were super guys to be able to hack living in the bush. We absolutely loved their attention.

The best night spots we were taken to were places called the Golden Dragon and the Bula Talei Club. Both were in downtown Suva. The "Dragon" as we called it, was a dank, stuffy den located above a Chinese restaurant. They had live bands that generally put out the latest rock and pop music. The place was usually packed with local girls, many of them obviously looking to be picked up. The cover charge for guys was $1.00, the girls got in free. We did go to the Dragon, usually with some of the girls introduced to us by our Suva friends. This way we could enjoy some drinking and dancing and not worry too much about who we were with.

The Bula Talei Club was a super nice place open to members only. Since our Suva friends belonged to the club, we usually got in by going with them or using their key to gain entry. The Bula Talei (Happy Time Club) provided live soft sensual music in a relaxed easy atmosphere. It was the type of place where you could really enjoy yourself. Compared to the Dragon, the Bula Talei was a much more casual quiet atmosphere. We spent several evenings there with some of our newly met friends in Suva. We certainly had nothing like this in Savusavu.

The journal entry for March 2, 1969, well summarizes our first few days of leave after Operation Play It Cool:

"These first three days have been filled with meeting friends, both old and new. Places like the Peace Corps Office, Waimanu Guest House,

Victoria Arcade, the Golden Dragon, and drunk two nights already! And some rather good meals...and plenty of beautiful girls!"

Probably the highlight of our leave times to Viti Levu were the visits we made to our friends James and Nuku Makasiale. After leaving Savusavu, James was posted as agriculture officer to Sigatoka, a small town on the southern coast of Viti Levu and located due west of Suva some 75 miles.

After spending a few days in Suva at the beginning of our leave, we would pack our gear and head out to Sigatoka. It was a grueling three- or four-hour bus ride from Suva along the winding coastal road. The busses on Viti Levu were like the old jungle busses in Savusavu, only bigger. On the bumpy dusty road to Sigatoka, we would get covered with a heavy layer of dust and grime. But the good times we had in Sigatoka were worth enduring the long ride.

As usual, James and Nuku welcomed us with open arms and open hearts. They were simply terrific people all over again. They eagerly looked forward to having the "Cakaudrove Boys" come to stay with them.

I remember clearly after arriving in Sigatoka and finding our way to the agriculture office and our first sight of Big James after such a long time. James saw us coming in and came out of his office, "Hey you guys," he said, "long time no see!" We shook hands all around and James said, "Nuku and I were wondering when you were coming down. We have been looking forward to having you three guys here." To Dave, Charlie, and I, we knew we would have an enjoyable stay in Sigatoka.

After James took us to his home, we showered and relaxed for a while. We then got aboard the Land Rover and were treated to a tour of the magnificent Sigatoka Valley, Fiji's premier farming area. The Sigatoka Valley is a very fertile region, producing large crops of potatoes, tobacco, and a wide variety of fruits and vegetables. It was a typically lush verdant landscape as our Land Rover climbed the hills on either side of the river valley. Compared to the Vanua Levu we knew, Sigatoka was a highly developed versatile agricultural region.

After arriving back home in late afternoon, we relaxed and waited for our beloved "Aunt Nuku" to come home. Nuku worked at the local government Fijian Native Land Board Office. When Nuku got home and came through the door we all shouted, "Bula Nuku!" She was all smiles as she said, "Isa, you boys made it down to Sigatoka." Charlie, Dave, and I proceeded to give Nuku a big hug and kiss. It was so good to be in James and Nuku's company once again.

We usually timed our visits to Sigatoka on weekends so that James and Nuku could throw a big party. They never disappointed us for we always had a big bang-up party that was a smashing success. Nuku of course would outdo even herself by providing plenty of good food.

During the March 1969, visit to their home, we planned a big party and included many Peace Corps Volunteers from the area. Of course, our old buddies, Ron Moore, and Reggie Berry, were there as well as several newer Volunteers from the recently arrived Fiji II group. We Volunteers bought the booze for the party.

Along with Peace Corps people, our party swelled in numbers because James would often invite many local people as well. Our parties began early and ended late, usually when the booze finally ran out or when everyone had passed out, whichever occurred first.

James' house would be a frenzy of activity and loud music during one of our parties. James, having spent time in Hawai`i going to school, loved to party, and loved dancing music. He had a terrific record collection and a good stereo system. We would put the records on and dance the night away, getting drunk in the process.

One amusing incident I recall took place just about the time one of our parties was to begin in early evening. James had gone out earlier for something and was a little late in returning. Many guests had begun arriving in the meantime and everyone was wondering where Big James was. Suddenly, in through the door staggers loveable Big James, smiling and carousing. Obviously, he had not waited for the party to start. He was sailing high already.

Big James, full of fun and mischief, hollered at us, "Hey, you guys! Wow, I'm smashed!"

We all broke up over that. Charlie shot back at James, "Hey James, where have you been? We've been waiting for you to start the party."

And James smiling said, "Oh, I already started the party down at the hotel." James had met a couple of friends at the hotel while we were making all the preparations for the party at his house.

In true Fijian style, as only Big James could do it, he came to his own party a bit tipsy from the start. It was simply James' way of getting a party off to a flying start. By the time the evening was over, almost everyone was smashed like James. Parties at James and Nuku's house were always smashing successes.

Inasmuch as we looked forward to our leaves in Suva, there were times when the big city hung heavy on us. A letter from Dave to his family on March 3, 1969, explains:

"...I am writing from the South Pacific Guest House here in Suva. Got here on February 27 after five months and three weeks in the villages and hills of Cakaudrove. It's nice to be where you can find electricity, western and Chinese food, cars, movies, etc. Trouble is the noise level seems incredible after Vanua Levu."

So, there were adjustments we had to make upon getting back to the city, but it did not take us long. We enjoyed our leave times to the fullest and they usually passed by quickly. Before we knew it, it was time to be heading back to Savusavu. At times, we had mixed emotions about returning. We were torn between wanting to go back to Vanua Levu and wanting to stay in Suva.

During the first year's leave it was easier to return to Vanua Levu because we knew we had a job to complete, the agriculture census. However, in March 1969, we had even graver doubts about returning since our future was somewhat uncertain. We were not sure what our roles were to be now that the census would be complete.

For this reason, we had even more second thoughts. But in the end the return to Vanua Levu won out. We knew we at least had a place in Cakaudrove, and we had established incredible rapport and a fine working relationship with the people. These factors were too heavy to turn away from. We knew that we had to return to Savusavu. That was our place.

And so, our long-awaited leaves came to an end. We returned to Savusavu on Sunday, March 16, 1969. The journal entry for March 19th summarizes my feelings about our leave:

"Anyway, these last two weeks were filled with quite a lot, mainly fun and a different atmosphere, away from the bush. There were sights of Suva revisited, the noises of a city, a nice place to just dump your weary bod, having what you wanted, beer, chow (love that Chinese food!) , and lots of pretty girls.

James and Nuku Makasiale and their warmth, Ron and Reggie, Bob Dawdy, and the rest of the Peace Corps crowd down on Viti Levu. Talking over beer in the new Suva Travelodge, a beautiful hotel; a party in Sigatoka, in our pad in Suva, at the Dragon, the flicks, and many girls! Booze and broads galore!

So many things that I remember from that great vacation, one of the swingingest two weeks I've ever had in my life."

We returned to Vanua Levu, physically and spiritually refreshed. We were now ready to confront our future, the last eight months of our two-year service. In all the period leading up to the end of the census we were never given any idea as to what we would be doing during this last stage of our service.

Charlie, Dave, and I were somewhat apprehensive about the prospects. Our future in Cakaudrove was up in the air and we were not certain what would happen.

CHAPTER 11

AN UNCERTAIN TIME

For over a year now, Charlie, Dave and I had been living and working in the bush country of Cakaudrove Province. We had successfully completed an exceedingly difficult project: the very first census of agriculture in all the province, part of a countrywide effort. We were now ready for something else.

We had proven ourselves capable of handling living and working in the bush. We had learned the language, gotten to know the people in our respective areas, and survived a rigorous existence. We had shown that we were capable of handling any job given us.

With our year's experience behind us, we felt that we could now function well enough to be what the Peace Corps called "agents of change." But the apprehension we carried regarding our future roles after the census was completed began to slowly prove justified.

After our arrival back in Savusavu from our Suva leaves, we met with our boss, Josua Cavalevu, the agriculture officer for the province. Our purpose in meeting with Joe was to discuss our future roles. The journal entry for March 19, 1969, provides a prelude to the next several months:

141

"…Monday it was a meeting with Josua concerning what we'll be doing the rest of this year. Boy! Talk about being up in the air. Looks like we'll have to find our own thing to do around here for the next eight months or so."

Joe was necessarily vague in his discussions with us regarding our future roles with the agriculture department. It was somewhat of a sticky problem, for the Fiji Department of Agriculture, the Peace Corps, and in particular, us, the Volunteers out in the field.

Much of this we learned toward the end of our service through the final termination meetings and conferences. At the time we were quite in the dark as to what was happening to us.

What it boiled down to was this: the Fiji Department of Agriculture didn't really know what they were going to do with us after the census was completed. They had no plan for us. This situation arose from the fact that most of the agriculture volunteers were in fact not trained in agriculture. Most of us, including Charlie, Dave and me, were liberal arts graduates. Our so-called agriculture training in Hawai`i was wholly inadequate and certainly didn't make us experts in tropical agriculture.

Part of the situation, as we learned much later, was due to the fact that our Peace Corps program suffered from poor planning. Fiji was promised some agriculture experts. What they got was us. In the process of realizing this, we ended up working on the agriculture census for a year or so and were then relegated to an uncertain status where our roles with the department were really unsure. It was a situation where no one was to blame and yet somewhere in the bureaucracy, a bad decision was made or something wasn't communicated well. At any rate, we were the guys who were stuck in the middle.

As the last eight months of our service went along, it became more and more obvious that our skills were being wasted. We were at the point where we were readily known and accepted by the people, we were part of their community, and we knew the culture intimately. And yet we had no real job, even though we were still attached to the agriculture department.

It became increasingly apparent to us that we would have to fend for ourselves and become self-starting. We would have to create our own jobs, roles, and responsibilities. It was a difficult thing to do after working under the organizational structure of the census work.

There were some real attempts at productive work over the next several weeks and months. Some of the projects we became involved with were individual efforts and some were team efforts. One such team project that Dave and I became involved in for a while was a time/man hours study. It dealt with determining the overall work production of individual and group farming efforts. We would go out into the field and observe farmers working, such as weeding their coconuts, planting crops, etc. We would then plot out the amount of work they did, square footage, and the time it took them to complete that work. These statistics were turned in to the agriculture officer who used them in correlating the effectiveness of various work production methods.

One of the benefits of the project was the chance to travel once again, this time to Rabi Island, home of the Banabans from Ocean Island in the Gilberts. It was Dave's first visit to Rabi and my return visit as I had spent several days there earlier working on the census.

We were accompanied by several members of the department staff from Savusavu who conducted a general extension tour. Dave and I did our time/man hours study on some coconut maintenance and grass planting demonstrations.

All in all, we spent a terrific four days on Rabi and received super hospitality as usual from the Banaban people. We were treated to some great food, grog parties, and on our last night a beautiful feast and a dancing program by the Banaban girls. It was simply a terrific trip, made easier by the project we worked on.

Another project that Dave and I became involved with was a mini-census of the cocoa production in Cakaudrove. A new cocoa research officer, Savenaca Railoa, had recently arrived at the Wainigata Cocoa Station near Savusavu. We knew Savenaca from previous meetings and we got along well with him. He seemed to feel that with our knowledge and experience gained from the census work, we could be useful in gathering more specific data on cocoa production throughout the province.

So, for several weeks Dave and I worked along with Savenaca compiling up-to-date production records on the cocoa farmers of the province. This cocoa survey work required that we spend time in the Savusavu main office, and the Wainigata Station, as well as touring through the main cocoa growing areas of Cakaudrove and visiting the farmers. On a few occasions, we even had to repeat some of the counting and measuring of cocoa groves in the field.

All in all, it was one of the few occasions in which one of the staff members of the department attempted to utilize our talents and skills on a productive project. To Savenaca, we were grateful that he at least attempted to get us involved in some productive work, even though it was a short term project.

During the time that Dave and I were busy with the time/man hours studies and the cocoa survey projects, Charlie wasn't exactly sitting down up in the bush country of Natewa Bay. Charlie had been a self-starter from the beginning. He was a highly motivated, knowledgeable fellow who utilized what he had learned from working on the census. He had made himself well known throughout his district of Vaturova and the people had come to place great trust and confidence in him.

This in turn had allowed Charlie to become more closely involved in his village community affairs. He became a director of the village cooperative store and was able to turn the store's success around. When he had first come to Korotasere, the store was in pretty bad financial condition and had few members supporting it. Through wise management, Charlie was able to improve the overall financial status of the cooperative and significantly boosted the supporters of the co-op venture in the village.

Charlie also became involved in cocoa production improvement. His area of Vaturova was a highly productive area for cocoa, an important cash crop. The area's isolation was compounded by a lack of roads. When harvested, the cocoa beans needed to be fermented on the spot, the first stage of curing the cocoa for market. For this reason, Charlie was instrumental in getting the agriculture department to build a cocoa fermenting dryer at Korotasere. This dryer significantly increased the farmers cash income as they decreased their cocoa bean loss due to spoilage. Once fermented and dried properly, the beans were shipped by boat to the Savusavu market.

Charlie's forte lay in his excellent relationship with the people of his area. Likewise, Dave and I had good rapport among the people in our respective areas. So, we began to rely on our own initiative to get involved with them.

One example of Dave's relatively successful involvement with his community was the Savusavu Jaycees Club. With this community service group, Dave became involved in some fund-raising fairs and events and even made a trip or two to Viti Levu on Jaycees business. Through this type of activity, Dave took on a more active and viable role in his community.

In my own village of Tukavesi, I took on a different project on my own. Partly through the requests of a couple of people in Tukavesi, I formed a class at the village school in English for Adults. Through popular demand, I decided to try a stint at being a teacher.

I went through the rudimentary planning stages, contacting the Peace Corps for help, materials, etc. and even gained the cooperation of the teachers at the village school. These two teachers, one was the headmaster (principal) agreed to give me all the help I needed in reaching out to the adults in the village. So, with everything ready, I began my first class on May 5, 1969. The journal describes the outcome:

"...And so tonight was the beginning of my community development work. I started an adult education course in English to help those that want to learn how to speak better English. It was an evening to remember because I was supposed to be helped by the schoolmasters here. Well, it turned out that they were both pretty smashed on a bottle of gin.

Boy! They were in no shape to try to teach anything. So, it was so typical of the crazy things that have happened to me here in Fiji. Anyway, I had my class, such as it was, and will try to carry on with more."

I returned to my bure that night and soberly contemplated what I should do. I decided to go ahead and the next day's journal entry, May 6, 1969, ends a little more positively:

"...Had my class again tonight. Quite a few more showed up. A pretty fair turnout, about 26 people. Still don't know how good this thing will turn out but I am going to give it what I've got. Certainly a chance to do something different and constructive."

The English class continued over the next several weeks. I held class a couple of nights per week on the average when I was in Tukavesi. Because I was still involved in agriculture department projects which required me to be away from Tukavesi, the class meetings and attendance gradually tapered off. However, I did meet with the class as often as I could and finally did get one of the teachers to do some of the teaching on his own. In fact, he conducted the class a few times while I was away. At other times, the class gradually shrunk enough that I held class meetings in my own house.

With these various projects we were able to gain some satisfaction and sense that we were making a contribution. Some of these projects were not exactly on a large scale but they were entirely our own attempts at community development, that catch all phrase for doing what we were doing. The Peace Corps must have been happy with us. Maybe we were becoming "agents of change" after all.

So, mostly through our own efforts, we became involved in various work projects. Still, it was not enough. Our generally unclear status caused some frustration. Even though we were doing things, we still had too much time on our hands and weren't involved in any concrete structured work routines. This was a most difficult thing to accept.

Out of this situation then arose something of a solution, however temporary. That was a self-immersion into the Fijian culture. Because of the amount of free time on our hands, we became more aware of the culture and relationships in which we lived and thus became more intimate with them. Probably without a doubt, the last eight months of our service in Cakaudrove saw us identify even more closely with the Fijian culture than at any other time.

This came about because of our skill and ability in the language and knowledge of the culture gained over the previous year. The yaqona drinking sessions, the village dances, the yarning sessions we shared with the people made us more Fijianized than ever before. In spite of our uncertain work roles, we profited enormously from our relationship with the people. During the last months of our service, this would have to take the place of the job satisfaction we so desperately craved and sought. For myself it was to be a bitter-sweet reward.

CHAPTER 12

A REAWAKENING

As the weeks passed by from April through August 1969, we were continually burdened by the dilemma of our situation. We had little of the concrete job satisfaction we wanted and saw limited success with our own individual projects.

Even though allusions were made to our being full-fledged officers of the agriculture department in Cakaudrove, it was not hard to separate myth from reality. In between work stints on the various projects we had going, time often hung heavy on our hands. There was a definite lack of something to do. I personally was bothered by the idea that I was wasting time and achieving little constructive work. I was restless.

Because of this situation, the three of us were more involved in the cultural aspects of our assignments. It seemed that we took more of an active interest in the various village dances, grog sessions, celebrations, and so on.

In Savusavu, where we often gathered for weekends, we usually managed to find a dance or a party to attend. Failing that, we bought a bottle of rum or whiskey and some beer and proceeded to get fantastically drunk.

One of our best friends, Lolohae Waqatabu, the head nurse at Savusavu Hospital, often took us under her protective wing. Lolo was a terrifically bright girl with an outgoing vibrant personality. She did her nursing training in Australia and was a highly articulate knowledgeable person. She was also a typical fun-loving Fijian. She was a beautiful woman as well. She always made us a part of any party or gathering planned up at the hospital or nursing quarters. The three of us guys had a rather notorious reputation for having a good time. Lolo looked on us with amusement and sometimes referred to us as her "three stooges." To her astonishment we lived up to that label by continually being the life of most parties and generating enthusiasm wherever we went.

Some of the best parties we attended were up at the Savusavu Hospital's staff quarters. The journal entry for August 4, 1969, notes one such party:

"...Had a great party Saturday night at the nurses' home at the hospital. Lolo, our real good friend, invited us up for a party after a big day of rugby games that afternoon. Man! What a wild night. We three guys came to that party completely smashed on a bottle of Bacardi Rum. Did we ever have a good time. We were really the life of that party as we were told yesterday. I hadn't had so much fun in a long time. That was the first party we had been to together in a long time. It was the first time we'd been drunk together too, in a long time."

Rugby, the British version of football, was played with a passion by the Fijians. Each village fielded a team during rugby season, composed of the young fellows of the village. On Saturdays in Savusavu, the town was filled with a carnival atmosphere as several teams from the surrounding area came in for games. We often went to the field to watch some of the tough hard-hitting action.

Charlie was the only one of us with guts enough to attempt playing. As another example of his fine community involvement, he tried out for and made the Vaturova rugby team from his area. As in everything, Charlie put his heart and soul into it and was the pride of his team.

On one weekend, Dave and I travelled up to Napuka Mission at the end of the Buca Bay road in my area to watch a rugby match between Tunuloa, the team from my area, and Vaturova, Charlie's team. We had a fun weekend, dancing and grogging the night away, after Vaturova soundly trounced Tunuloa.

It was at this gathering too, that Charlie and I did our version of the Great American Dance Contest. The Fijians of course loved dancing and it was a part of the festivities of this big rugby weekend at Napuka.

The mission hall was jammed packed with guys and gals from all over. The smell of talcum powdered bodies, coconut oil, and yaqona filled the air, along with the pungent aroma of Fiji tobacco. The guitars and ukuleles strummed up and began sending out a medley of island hits.

And since the Fijians liked competition so much, as witnessed by the rugby games earlier in the day, somebody hit upon the idea of having a dance contest. It was to be Vaturova against Tunuloa all over again. And who should they select but Charlie and me to be the contestants.

Charlie and I rose to the challenge, savoring the chance to show off a little. Charlie, of course, was an excellent dancer. No doubt about it, he had soul. But the kid from Iowa matched each movement as we twisted, swung, and moved around the hall to the delight of the audience. They shouted out their encouragement and support and seemed to enjoy the spectacle of the two Americans trying to outdo one another on the dance floor.

The band played through a series of hit tunes of the day. Charlie and I went through a couple of partners each as we continued to dance away.

Finally, reaching the end of our endurance, we called a truce, declared a standoff and were rewarded with a rousing round of applause and a big bowl of yaqona.

In typical Fijian fashion, we had stirred the hearts of the people and shown them once again that we enjoyed living with them and accepted their lifestyle. The people were delighted.

Vaturova won the rugby game that day but we as Americans and Volunteers, out hanging loose with the people as we so often did, won their hearts once again.

In late April 1969, as part of our job-related activity, Dave and I travelled to Taveuni Island for a staff meeting. Most of the Savusavu agriculture office staff was there as well. For some reason, probably a lack of transportation and/or communication, Charlie did not attend.

We were to spend a couple of days in meetings and field trips with Joe Cavalevu, the agriculture officer. As it turned out, our meetings were cut short on the second day as the boss did not show up for some unknown reason. Taking advantage of the situation in true Fijian style, we headed for the island's lone pub in the island's only tourist hotel.

The journal for April 28, 1969, notes:

"... Well, just as if it were straight out of a Michener story, we all got smashed, Dave and I and the staff. God! That Fiji Bitter Beer is strong! We finally had a chow in some guy's house after a lot of talking, arguing, etc. What a hell of a night."

It was after this drinking bout at Taveuni that Dave and I pulled what proved to be one of the most hilarious stunts our Fijian co-workers had ever seen. The Fijians, of course, drink to get drunk, no holds barred. And generally, in a pub, brawls and fights are commonplace, even among friends.

But the Fijians, tough and short tempered, can be equally loving and forgiving after a hard fight. So much so that in a complete reversal, drunken, slugging, swearing combatants one minute can be slobbering, forgiving, still drunk bosom buddies the next.

Such was the case when Dave and I decided to pull a fast one on the Fijians. We staged an incredible fake fight on the road outside the Taveuni pub.

As we exited from the pub, Dave and I began a pushing and shoving match which totally astonished the Fijians. Dave and I heartily put ourselves into it and must have made one hell of an impression. The poor Fijians were stunned. Here were the two American Peace Corps Volunteers, the best of friends under normal conditions, now violently flailing at one another in a drunken melee. They did not know what to do.

Finally, one of the fellows came up and tried to pull us apart, crying out, "Please, please, fellows don't do this. You may hurt each other. Oh, please stop this!"

At this, as if on cue, Dave and I stepped apart, arms around each other's shoulders crying and slobbering in typical Fijian fashion, "Oh my friend, what have we done?" and "Oh, my brother, are you OK?" and even "Oh, we are just brothers!"

Of course, these statements made in Fijian were aimed directly at our friends. At once they sensed that they had been taken hook, line, and sinker. Dave and I broke up with laughter and were soon followed by our friends, the Fijians.

On that day, our Fijian co-workers learned that the two Yankees could get drunk for the fun of it and even poke a little fun at that essentially very human being called a Fijian.

As a final note on that little stunt, the April 29, 1969, journal notes:

"Last night I was so bombed out that if a man hadn't shown me and Dave the road to our house, we'd probably never had found our way back.

On top of it, our house was not furnished at all, so we all sacked out on the floor. I only had a sulu (a wrap around lavalava) for a cover and my backpack for a pillow. Slept on the bare floor. How many times have I done that?"

It was about this time, April-May 1969, that the problem of our jobs or lack of them, took a turn for the worse. Joe Cavalevu, one of our language instructors in the Hawai`i training program and our immediate boss the past year in Cakaudrove, was transferred to the other side of Vanua Levu at Labasa as Senior Agriculture Officer for the entire Northern Division (which was all of the island of Vanua Levu). There was no replacement for his post of agriculture officer in Savusavu. With this, the department was left without leadership and Charlie, Dave and I were left dangling even further out on the proverbial limb.

The leadership of the Cakaudrove Agriculture Department was left to the subordinate field officers of each district, supposedly working cooperatively. We in turn were left in somewhat of a void and were made even more uncertain of our specific roles. This action built pressure and tension as the weeks went by.

The stress and strain of our uncertain situation is evident in the May 28th journal entry:

"...But here I am faced with a day to day life of little change, no real work to gain satisfaction from and the fact that I am getting a little tired of it all now, maybe what you call 'culture weariness'."

And even though there were things to find wrong with my situation, there was always something to find right with it too, as the journal for June 8, 1969, notes:

"Before I turn in for this day, no matter how bad things are here for me, many things I still enjoy experiencing. I still feel like I have accomplished a lot, even though maybe not in terms of work. I still like being here in Fiji. The stars are brilliant and beautiful in the Fiji sky tonight, as they are every night. This is just one of the things I really do enjoy—just looking up at the beautiful South Pacific sky and stars."

With our reduced job activity, time often hung heavy on our hands and we were caught in a confining routine existence. It has been written and said that for a western man, life in the South Pacific too often becomes confining, very routine, and devastatingly simple. It is all true as the following journal entries describe:

June 19, 1969:

"Tonight I went through the same ritual I've been going through all week long: cards about 4:00pm with Save, bath in the river, wait for supper, chow, rest and then cards again with both Save and Marama. Boy, talk about a routine, I guess this was just about the most routinized week I've had in a long time here in Fiji."

August 20. 969:

"It's a beautiful hot sunny day, a typical South Pacific day. I walked along the road, just thinking. Life here is just really hum-drum sometimes. There was the mangrove swamp along the road, the 'beaches' such as they are, and coconuts everywhere.

Many funny thoughts. I saw a boat following the coast of Kioa and remembered the days, the hot afternoons I spent there. I saw the SE coast of Cakaudrove, the lower side of Buca Bay, I saw Taveuni in the far distance and I thought of all the days I've spent in those areas, on days like today and on other kinds of days.

I thought of the people who live on the copra estates and villages. I thought of their very isolated, dull, routine, hum-drum type of life. For after all, that is the way the South Pacific and Fiji really is.

I walked along, through Diloi estate and thought how it would be to live for the rest of my life on a copra estate. Boy, I couldn't take it. I even met up with the part-European 'planter' of Diloi. I mean he's not that much of a big shot. Why hell, he was even cutting his own copra. He's just a co-conut farmer like the rest of these people here in Cakaudrove. Not even a farmer really, just a 'harvester,' goes around picking up nuts as they drop.

But anyway, it's a very simple, irregular type of life, and I am quite sure that I wouldn't want to stay here for the rest of my life. It's surely a humbling experience to live here for two years though."

Going into August 1969, Charlie, Dave, and I were anticipating our upcoming final leave time. Our last two weeks of leave would be taken in early September and in conjunction with a planned Peace Corps termination of service conference in Nadi. At that conference we planned to unload the anxieties and frustrations of our work situations in Cakaudrove.

Our leaves were everything we had expected them to be and more. We saw all our old friends among the Volunteers, visited James and Nuku Makasiale in Sigatoka, and Ron and Reggie as well. We had plenty of parties, good food, and booze. We even got a chance to discuss our situations with a couple of Peace Corps staff members from Washington, D.C. But our big break came with our visit to Sigatoka.

The journal for September 17, 1969, describes the situation:

"And now we face something of an opportunity and challenge. Looks like we three guys will be transferring to Viti Levu here around October 1st to work on marketing potatoes for Sigatoka Valley Co-op. Will work for Ron and Reg.

They suggested it, we responded in the affirmative and we are working to set up the transfer officially. And it looks definite right now. Charlie would be sent to Lautoka, Dave placed in Sigatoka, and I would be placed right here in Suva.

How about that! It is a great opportunity to get out of our situations there in Cakaudrove. We're really enthusiastic about the possibilities. Man, it's a very lucky break for us, after all the stuff we've put up with.

So anyway, our leave has been quite productive in many ways. All we have to do now is go back, get the final word, pack our things and be ready to move in two weeks."

It was all heady stuff for three guys that had spent over a year and a half in the bush of Cakaudrove. Somebody was offering us a real job in totally new surroundings. I for one was terribly excited about the prospects and allowed my spirits to soar incredibly high.

We thought it would be only a formality to push through a transfer for us. But we did not realize how slowly the wheels turned or failed to turn at all. I allowed the excitement and anticipation to drive up the tension and practically made myself a nervous wreck. I also let it interfere with my judgment and nearly made some disastrous decisions.

The September 19, 1969, journal notes:

"We still received no final word from Suva regarding our transfer and things are looking somewhat pessimistic. Someone in the Agriculture Department may be against this move. And if it doesn't come through, well I'll be at my wit's end and don't know what I'll do."

Among the alternatives I considered at this time were to transfer to Suva as planned; ask Peace Corps for another job entirely; just go to Suva, terminate, and go back to the States; and just stick it out up in Cakaudrove and finish out the last two months there.

The journal for September 19, 1969, continued with an ominous note on how desperate I felt at the time:

"I've got to face it. I have no job or work to do. Everybody knows it, we've talked about it, analyzed it, and so on, and it still comes out to equal zero. I still have no job in Cakaudrove Agriculture Department this very day. And I am just fed up with it. I want something different. I feel like I've pretty much decided to do something about my situation here, one way or the other."

The next few days saw no improvement in the situation. If nothing else, the tension grew, and nerves grew more taunt. The journal for September 21, 1969, notes:

"I did some very deep thinking and considering. I believe now that I must get out of Cakaudrove altogether, especially Buca Bay. I've written Peace Corps a letter asking for a transfer or an early termination from service. This of course depends on whether our transfer to Sigatoka comes through or not. I really feel now that I must get out of here. I can't stand the sitting around I've been doing here at Buca Bay."

During these days I tried to occupy myself with some of the cocoa production survey work Dave and I had been doing previously. During the week of September 22-27, I went down to Wainigata Cocoa Station, did some work, and returned to Buca Bay. The journal entry for September 27, 1969, describes my reaction to the request for transfer denial we received:

"As things turned out, we didn't get the transfer to Sigatoka as expected. To make a long story short, I was in a rather high state of tension, anger, bitterness, and frustration all week long. I think it's one reason why I came down sick—the flu or something.

Well, I called and wrote Peace Corps and told them I wanted out of here. I told Dave and Charlie that I had to get out of Cakaudrove. I went through too much emotional stress and strain in this week, more than I ever had before in Fiji."

As the next few days passed by, I gradually got more of a hold on myself and the situation in general. The September 30th, 1969, journal notes:

"I guess I've cooled off somewhat about the general situation and am content to just settle down here at Buca Bay for the rest of the time. I still can't relate like I used to be able to but guess I'll have to do my best."

So, reluctantly, we faced our final two months of service in Cakaudrove thinking of what might have been down in Sigatoka with our friends James and Nuku, and Ron and Reggie. All these people too were disappointed when they found out we would not be coming to Sigatoka. Even our very good friend, Lolo, who had transferred to Sigatoka a couple of months earlier and whom we saw on our September leave was disappointed. Because with that circle of friends, who now knew each other as well, we were planning on a fine final couple of months before we finished our service in December.

However, out of this entire episode came a strong message, a message that we had accomplished quite a lot, more perhaps than any of us had even thought possible. The message came from our very dearest friend, Lolo, now the head nurse in Sigatoka. Lolo wrote to me when she found out that I was near quitting and leaving Cakaudrove.

However, she wrote concerning the three of us, the Cakaudrove Team, Charlie, Dave and me.

Her letter is dated, Tuesday, September 30, 1969:

"...please John, don't give it up. You've only got two more months to finish up that marvelous relationship you have established with the people of Cakaudrove. You'll only spoil the reputation of your people— Americans as a whole—with us.

As you know very well, that Peace Corps all over Fiji are very well liked by my people. For Fijians (who have hardly any chance of living with a white man—talking, joking, grog sessions, etc.) that matters most. (Just two more months.)

We have all built ourselves to a certain point of your coming over and started to imagine all the fabulous times we're going to have, and then bang! was the anti-climax. So emotionally we all got upset. It's the emotion you've got to fight against, not the people!!!"

That was probably the most convincing, persuasive, and touching letter I have ever received. And coming from a Fijian whom I admired, respected, and loved so very much, it struck a chord in my heart and soul. My decision to "stick it out" up in Cakaudrove was reconfirmed, my faith in what I was doing here in Fiji, my real role as a Peace Corps Volunteer, rekindled with hope.

To this day, I am indebted to Lolo for helping bring me back to my senses and realize what I had going for me in Cakaudrove. With her message in mind, I faced the final weeks of my service with renewed determination.

CHAPTER 13

ON BEING FIJIAN

During the two years we lived in the villages of Cakaudrove, we learned what it was like to live as a Fijian. Besides a real learning experience, it was at the same time a very sobering and humbling one. Fiji, being an essentially communal culture taught us how to live with and for others. It was something we rarely encounter in our self-centered western culture.

Throughout our travels and experiences, we gained tremendous insight and understanding of that most wonderful human being called a Fijian. The average Fijian villager lived a very simple life style with simple wants and needs.

A reflection of their simple life is aptly described in a letter from Dave to his family, dated August 10, 1969:

"...Here in Fiji people play cards and other simple games and thus relate to each other. In western society, people are too often isolated and alienated in their social life...Almost all social activities (here) have involved person to person relations. Whether it's playing cards, having a talanoa, or even watching a rugby game. This is the greatest difference between Fijian and western society...In Fijian village or communal life it's people doing things together, albeit simple things....There are simple joys, simple chores, and simple sorrows. The people have parties, dances, and yaqona sessions. The farmers cut the copra and the women wash clothes and bear children. And the old rest and die."

Dave offers further insight into the average Fijian man in the following excerpts from a letter home, dates March 19, 1969:

"The Fijian is a damn nice guy. He's usually about 5'9" tall, weighs about 165 lbs., pretty heavy alright. He's friendly, has a good sense of humor, jokes very simple, phony, but never insulting or revolting.

Eats mostly tavioka, taro, boiled taro leaves, and coconut milk and fish...big smile, often a manly mustache, fantastic physiques. Always very humble and sometimes fearful when he first meets a white man... if old enough, constantly hearkens back to the glory days of World War II when he fought alongside Lucky Strike smoking Americans at Guadalcanal and Bougainville or knew GI's in Suva.

Tells you Americans are much more friendly and fair than are the English, New Zealanders or Aussies...If he drinks, he drinks only to get drunk, and does so with famous bouts. Always asks you about Clay, Patterson, 'Roko' Marciano (Rocky)...smokes incredibly strong twist tobacco in cigar form or in cigarettes rolled on the spot from newspaper.

If he comes to your house, he'll ask you how much everything costs, which will irritate you. He'll also take every cigarette you offer him. You'll be giving cigarettes away all the time. That's an American custom he found out about in World War II.

Though he's only a farmer, he never talks about farming. Only wants to talk about daily life, small talking. Only English he knows may be the word 'OK.' If he can speak English, has a British accent.

...He has only one basic mood, carefree friendliness. He's not a moody guy and is rarely sad. Very musical and often good with a guitar...Feels isolated in his bush village. Wishes government officials visited more often. No business sense at all. Never saves his money.

There are probably a lot of traits I left out especially the deeper ones...Fijians' attitudes toward 'westerners' is one of the main things you have to deal with...The average Fijian is not stupid and his view is generally a more sophisticated one than given credit for...you must show to the people that you respect their culture and intend to work with them and not on them...Learn their language and just be a nice guy and you'll have it made...He's a pretty nice guy and will help you if you know him."

One of the most important survival skills that we learned was, of course, the language. Soon after our arrival in Cakaudrove, we found out how essential it was to work on learning how to speak the language. We had been trained in Hawai`i in the Fijian dialect of Bauan, the main dialect of spoken Fijian.

However, we soon found out that Bauan was quite different from the dialect of Cakaudrove. In fact, within Cakaudrove there were sub-dialects in the various districts of the province. While we could get along quite well in the use of Bauan, the three of us soon discovered that it would be beneficial to learn the local dialects as well.

While we may not have been completely proficient in the use of the Cakaudrove dialects, we did very well in acquiring a high level of proficiency in standard Bauan. Our facility in the language was perhaps our single most outstanding characteristic and was proof positive of the intimate knowledge and relationship we had developed on the job.

During one of our early leaves to Suva we were given a follow up language test by one of our former training instructors. The test was to see how much growth we had made in language use. The three of us passed with very high marks. We always prided ourselves on being among the best speakers in comparison to the other Volunteers, many of whom never became very proficient because of their various job assignments.

The fact that we were placed in a position where we had to learn and use the language was crucial to our success. Many Volunteers placed in town and city environments could get by in English on the job and thus never really had to learn the language. Not so for us.

Another aspect of language was the Pidgin English used throughout Cakaudrove. It seemed pidgin was especially strong in Buca Bay, my area. The pidgin was a combination of Fijian-English. There were several people in Buca Bay who frequently used this in conversation with me and I eventually acquired some skill in it. Many times the people using pidgin were trying to show off their skill in English, to my amusement.

Among the many cultural phenomena to which we were exposed, none was more endearing than that of drinking yaqona. In much of Polynesia and Melanesia, yaqona or kava drinking is a traditional sacred ritual reserved for chiefs and only on ceremonial occasions.

In Fiji, yaqona or "grog" drinking is as much a part of the culture as eating and sleeping and often times more important than either. Yaqona is made from the *piper methysticum* plant, a member of the pepper family. The stalks and roots are generally pounded to a pulp and then mixed with water to produce a distinctly aromatic muddy looking concoction. Usually mixed in a large carved wooden basin called a "tanoa," it was served up in a half coconut shell "bilo" or cup.

It was usually drunk in large quantities over several hours' duration. Usually it was a real social affair, either with some friends and neighbors gathered around the yaqona bowl exchanging stories and news in the evening or it would be at a village dance and "gunu penny," a fund raiser where bowls of grog were bought for a penny or two each.

But whatever the occasion, grog drinking was a serious traditional custom. It was the national pastime. For the simple living village folks it was the one activity they had that provided social interaction and entertainment.

Grog, not an alcoholic beverage, was soporific. Drunk in huge quantities, it could make you drowsy and melancholy and led to listlessness, inactivity and loss of appetite. To an extent it was addictive and some actually became dependent on it.

Taking part in all night grog sessions gave the Volunteer out in the field instant rapport in the village. There were many times in my travels that I went for days on end reeling from one grog session to another.

The journal for August 24, 1969, notes:

"Save and the school teachers came around with some grog yesterday afternoon and evening. My Lord, that makes six days or nights in a row that I've been drinking that stuff."

Grog sessions were often held in a bure or house. A grog session was often accompanied with card playing or checkers and even caroms. At other times, if it was a dance and grog session, it would be in the village school or a "vaka tunuloa," a simple shed made of a wood pole frame with corrugated metal roofing and coconut thatched walls.

If it was a village dance, there was a need for lots of room as the place would soon fill up with wall to wall bodies, mostly village girls. The dances were incredible affairs where the girls would dress up in their best dress and even wear fragrant toilet water and powder. The guys would often come in their best long pants and a colorful flowered print "Bula" shirt.

The music would be provided by a small combo of five or six guys picking on a various assortment of guitars and ukuleles. They would sing and pick their way through a variety of Fijian pop songs and even American pop tunes of the day. Most of the dancing was initiated by the girls. They usually got up and went to the boys and invited them to dance. It was different than the American boy ask girl arrangement.

By tradition, a Fijian village dance would not be complete without some drunks. There would usually be a handful or more of the guys who would get tanked up on a nefarious thing called "home brew." Traditional yaqona was not enough for these guys. Keeping in mind that Fijians drink to get drunk, this is what "home brew" was all about.

The formula for making and using home brew was something like this: take one five gallon biscuit tin, add water, yeast, sugar. Wait a couple of hours and drink. Get really drunk. Go to the dance and fight. Get sick. Throw up. Pass out.

One of Dave's letters aptly describes a typical Fijian party's ending, dated December 29, 1968:

"The party ended in a brawl between two Fijians and two part-Europeans. Yuk! It was Savusavu back to normal."

The one and only time I ever tried home brew quickly made me swear off it forever. Dave and I were passing by the hospital staff quarters in Savusavu one night. At one house, there was much loud music and noise and we figured that they must be having a party or something. Well, one of the fellows who knew us came running out with a couple of cups full of home brew for us. He practically begged us to drink up and join the party. We had learned to avoid these types of situations especially when home brew was involved.

Well, we thought, we'll be nice guys and at least drink up the brews he brought to us. Dave and I downed the brew and continued on out the road to his place which was a couple of miles away. About half way there, both of us were suddenly attacked with severe cramping pains in the stomach and we staggered on out to his place. There we collapsed in agony. We spent the rest of the night retching in pain. Fortunately, nothing else came of the episode except a confirmed oath to never drink home brew again.

It seemed that whenever the Fijians whipped up a batch of home brew there were sure to be a bunch of drunks staggering around. A sure sign that a home brew session was on occurred when a Fijian came up to you and asked, "Sa via vodo Fiji Airways?" (Do you want to ride Fiji Airways?)

This of course was an allusion to the exhilarating high achieved from the home brew. True to form, the Fijians took off and were soon flying from the effects of the dastardly home brew. But in the same vein, they soon ended their flight with a violent gut-wrenching crash landing. It was an experience we learned to avoid at all costs.

Another popular, and dangerous drink that some Fijians imbibed in was methylated alcohol or spirits. This liquid was usually sold and used for use with Coleman lanterns. But somewhere along the line, some Fijian learned to drink it in order to get a quick satisfactory high on. Unfortunately for the Fijians, meth or spirits also wreaked havoc with things like kidneys and hearts and other internal organs. In spite of the dangers, many young Fijians often drank the stuff just to get drunk. Despite their seemingly peaceful nature, some Fijians just like getting drunk enough to risk themselves.

Another cultural aspect of Fiji that was somewhat inconspicuous but nonetheless endemic to the South Pacific was the Chinese shopkeeper. In all the stories of mankind, it is perhaps the Chinese shopkeeper's life on a remote South Pacific island which is seldom told. Even in the most remote isolated areas of Cakaudrove, one could always find a small general store run by a Chinese. Perhaps like no one else, the Chinese shopkeeper suffers silently in cultural and ethnic isolation.

Take for example Wing Tong. Here is a man in his early 50's who emigrated from China almost 20 years ago. He landed in Fiji with a meager amount of money and big dreams. Through connections made in China, and maybe some distant relatives in Suva or elsewhere, he was set up to become a trader and shopkeeper in the remote Wailevu area of Cakaudrove.

And there he was when I found him. Walking through the remote bush land of Wailevu on Operation Play It Cool, I chanced upon the "Chinaman's store" as the Fijians called Wing Tong Store. Here was Wing, living in what was for him total cultural isolation, far from any vestige of his homeland or people in a remote part of Fiji. It truly must have been a humbling experience to face one's entire existence under such circumstances.

But Wing Tong was surviving. In 20 years he had learned the language well, had built a good relationship and trade with the villagers of the area, had acquired a Chinese bride through the "China pipeline" and was raising a flock of youngsters.

Wing was typical of the Chinese traders who made it to the hinterlands of the South Pacific to establish their stores and dynasties. Throughout Fiji and all the South Pacific islands, there is always a Chinaman and a store somewhere back in the bush selling kerosene, sugar, salt, soap, tobacco, tea, and all the other necessities to the villagers.

Often times these men would live, work, and die, nameless and forgotten souls in the backwaters of the island world. My journal for August 25, 1969, mentions one such lost soul:

"...There was an old Chinese man who died today in the village, so they had the mourning period for him tonight. So I went down with

Filo and Marama and took part in some more grog drinking, which is traditional at times like this.

It's interesting because this old Chinaman used to be the shopkeeper here in Tukavesi for many years. So when he died, he had no relatives and was being cared for by the people here. So these people, so much very human, gave the poor old man a decent burial.

This is just the type of story, the old Chinese shopkeeper in the South Pacific islands, about whom James Michener would write. It's all part of the history, color, and background of the South Pacific. I'd never even met or knew the old guy myself. He just moreorless died as an unknown, except to the people of this village."

Events like weddings, funerals, holidays and other celebrations were often welcome affairs. For one reason, they usually meant a big feast or two plus the usual all night grog sessions and dances as well.

But it was the feasts that people, including us Volunteers living out in the villages, really looked forward to. Most of us were too often weary of the daily diet of fish (often canned mackerel), dalo, tavioka, and occasional canned corned beef. At a feast, be it a wedding, funeral or holiday, a head of cattle was often slaughtered and perhaps a pig was brought back from the forest. Also, there would be chicken, rice, and if one was really lucky, even pudding and cake. So when these rare occasions came your way, you took advantage of them.

The journal for July 6, 1969, describes one such occasion:

"Sunday I felt very tired but attended another big chow in Savusavu put on by Remi and Mela, Dave's neighbors. Two big feasts in two days—it's really great and happens rarely here in Fiji. You're lucky if you get that kind of eating once in 3-4 months. Man! All kinds of beef, pig, goat curry, fish, dalo, waci and cakes. Really enjoy getting away from the tin fish and tavioka of the daily diet."

There were even feasts for unusual or unexpected events, such as is explained in this journal entry for January 20, 1969:

"Tonight, a surprise. A great feast in the village for, of all things, celebration of a young boy's circumcision! But anyway, for his pains, I got a great feed tonight."

As great as it was to be invited to a feast, one thing was for certain, and that was that you were always welcome to come and eat in a Fijian's house. It didn't matter whether you were a friend or a stranger. Fijian custom dictated welcoming you into the house to rest and eat.

Among the many things the three of us guys did, perhaps none endeared us more to our Fijian friends more or captured the frivolity and humor with which we approached our situation than the Great Bread Eating Contest.

Midway in our second year of service, we were at Dave's place for a weekend. In Savusavu of course, fresh bread from the Chinese bakery was a luxury we seldom got out in the villages. Dave's neighbors, Mela and Remi, happened to be gone that particular weekend. Come Sunday morning, we had to make a fire and fix our own tea. We had a couple of loaves of bread we had picked up in town the day before.

Peni, another of Dave's neighbors, joined us for morning tea. The four of us were sitting there enjoying the fresh bread with canned margarine and jam. Peni, kept repeating the usual Fijian expression to "Gunu tea vaka levu" meaning to please drink and eat plenty.

And then it all seemed to start, like so many things, spontaneously. Dave said, "Oh, I've already had two cups of tea and four slices of bread."

Then Charlie said, "Well, I've had two cups of tea and five slices of bread."

Sensing the chance to show off, I boldly proclaimed, "Well, I've had two cups and six slices of bread."

That seemed to set it off. Soon we were grabbing slices of bread and pouring more tea, hoping to stay ahead of the next guy.

Dave said, "Geez, I've had eight pieces of bread."

Charlie announced, "Hey, I'm up to ten."

And I chimed in with "I'm still ahead, I've had eleven pieces."

Peni laughed and said encouragingly, "Io, gunu tea vaka levu!" meaning to drink and eat more.

Dave faded away from the challenge in a short while. He was satisfied with watching Charlie and I make fools of ourselves. Charlie and I continued to match each other, slice of bread for slice of bread. We were engaged now in mortal combat to the final inglorious end.

Twelve. Thirteen, Fourteen. The number of slices of bread went up and up. Both Charlie and I were becoming bloated and stuffed from tea and bread. Peni and Dave were sitting on the sidelines splitting their guts with laughter.

But I was bound and determined to not be outdone. Charlie kept goading me further. He was still only one piece of bread behind me. The number went to fifteen. And sixteen. The tension kept building. Who would quit first?

Both of us were completed stuffed. I picked up my seventeenth slide of bread, buttered it and managed to stuff it down. Charlie finished his last piece, I thought his sixteeth. He finally said, "OK, John, you win. I can't eat anymore."

And then he dropped the bomb on me. "Hey," he said, "that was really only my tenth slice of bread. I didn't really eat sixteen like I said. I was just leading you on to see how much you could eat!"

Everybody broke up in laughter. I was practically too full to laugh but considering that I had just been taken in I could hardly restrain laughing at myself. We kidded ourselves about our Great Bread Eating Contest and how I won it by eating seventeen slices of bread.

The next day, the news of our big contest was all over town, among the people we know. Many people stopped us and said they had heard about our "gunu tea contest." When Mela and Remi returned the first thing we heard was that they knew about our bread eating contest.

The Fijians loved it. They thought it was something for three Americans to sit in a bure having a bread eating contest.

We got a lot of laughs and more importantly, much endearment, out of that little episode. We never forgot the humorous results of our Great Bread Eating Contest.

Perhaps the biggest cultural event that Dave, Charlie and I witnessed in Fiji was the Vaka-Tara-i-Sulu, in honor of the late Tui Cakau, the paramount chief of Cakaudrove Province. This event took place in July, 1969, to officially close the mourning period for the deceased Tui Cakau.

It was a huge celebration that was laden with traditional symbolic and ceremonial significance. Thousands of people gathered at Somosomo, Taveuni. They came from all over Fiji to pay traditional homage to the new Tui Cakau. For the tribes of Cakaudrove, it was the time when they pledged their loyalty and allegiance to the new Tui or king.

During the time that we were there, we learned that this may well be the last time that such an event would be held due to the extreme cost of such an affair. The entire affair was spread over several days with much dancing, celebrating, feasts, grog sessions and more.

There was an outpouring of homage in the form of gifts, lengths of cloth and masi (tapa cloth), food, cattle, horses, pigs, dances, and more. It was a completely spectacular event, the likes of which are rarely seen anywhere.

Dave and I had gone to Taveuni as the invited guest of Savenaca Railoa, the research officer at Wainigata Cocoa Station. Charlie went to this event as a member of Korotasere's traditional meke dancing group.

Charlie's group had been practicing their dances for several months in anticipation of the celebration. For Charlie, it was a thrill and an honor to be the only American dancer performing in the Vaka Tara-i-Sulu.

The journal for July 19, 1969, describes my thoughts about what I had seen on Taveuni:

"I just returned from Taveuni and witnessing one of the biggest events in Fijian culture. The lifting of the mourning for the late chief of Cakaudrove, plus the honoring of the King of Fiji, the Vunivalu Bau.

Dave and I stayed with the chiefly people of Bau and Tailevu and saw all the events connected with this spectacle. It was really something. Somosomo was really jammed with people everywhere. There was much feasting and grogging. Dave and I slept wherever we could, usually in a pavilion type shelter, or vaka tunuloa, an open-air bamboo pavilion.

The grandeur and glory was tremendous, with people going all out, presenting tabuas, masi, mats, kerosene, livestock, food, etc. Then the mekes, dancing and everything else that goes with the event.

Charlie did the spear dance meke with his Korotasere group and was really the center of attraction and attention. Everyone raved about Charlie and he really did do well in his meke. The three of us had a good time around the place there too."

A letter Dave wrote to his family also sums up what we experienced on Taveuni. Dave's letter is dated July 24, 1969:

"We were in Somosomo, Taveuni, for the big traditional ceremony, the Vaka-Tara-i-Sulu, to commemorate one year since the king of Cakaudrove, Ratu Josefa Lalabalavu, died in March, 1968.

In a village of 350, over 4.000 people came from many provinces of Fiji. The Vunivalu, the King of Fiji, was there as was Ratu Sir

Kamisese Mara, the Chief Minister and ruling head of the Alliance Party.

Savenaca Railoa arranged so that John and I shook hands with the Vunivalu, Ratu George Cakobau. The two and a half day ceremony in which thousands of dollars worth of gifts and food were given was incredible.

There was also a long series of mekes, native dances. The meke groups came from different areas of Cakaudrove and Fiji. Charlie danced the meke wesi with the men from his area, using a long spear and a traditional fierce looking costume. He got his name on Radio Fiji for that and Ratu Penaia, the second highest chief in Cakaudrove gave him a special gift. It was the first time in history an American had danced at an ancient style ceremony.

John and I were made guests of some of the royal ladies. We had beef and taro for three days."

CHAPTER 14

UNFORGETTABLE CHARACTERS OF FIJI

The Peace Corps experience is by nature a people to people interchange where the volunteer and those he lives with share a great deal of their personal lives. Essentially then, the experience especially in Fiji, was woven around other people. Charlie, Dave, and I came to be the best of friends because our common experiences solidified the bonds of friendship. We shared so much together and with the people as well.

From these common experiences, the three of us came to know each other very well. We also came to know intimately many colorful and unforgettable characters which are so much a part of the South Pacific scene. For as it is the world over, the people are the real heart and soul of what Fiji is all about.

This chapter is devoted to some of those people who in one way or another touched our lives in Fiji. Because of the unique experiences we shared with these people, our adventure was made a little bit better.

There is only one word to describe a six-foot, 250 lb. Fijian with a goatee beard, and that is impressive. James Makasiale, our friend "Big James" was just that and more. In his early 30's, he was a very impressive figure, close cropped beard and all. He carried his bulk well.

James was a Fijian from the eastern Lau Islands. He looked more like a Polynesian than a Melanesian. He was the son of a provincial leader. He had graduated from the University of Hawai`i's East-West Center with a degree in Tropical Agriculture, one of few Fijians at that time who had a college education. James liked Americans and was very pro-Peace Corps.

When we first met James on the Suva wharf just before leaving for Vanua Levu in early 1968, it was friendship at first sight. At the time, we did not know how valuable, close, and lasting this new friendship would be. It would last throughout our two years of service. James had a natural, easy going, friendly disposition.

James was very serious about his work as temporary agriculture officer in Cakaudrove. He also felt that we could make a positive contribution and succeed in our roles as Volunteers. As our friend, James helped us considerably in the early months when we worked under him. He helped ease us into the roles we played and into the culture. He explained things concerning customs, language, and a host of other things we questioned. He wanted to see us succeed and did his best to give us a helping hand. He knew the culture shock we were experiencing as he himself had gone through it when he went to Hawai`i to study.

As serious as James was, he knew how to let it all out, relax, and have a good time. True to his Fijian nature, he liked having a rousing good time. That usually meant a wild round of drinking, either Fijian grog or booze.

It was James in fact, who gave us our initial baptisms in the fine art of grog drinking. During the first few weeks in Savusavu, after working hours, we often gathered around the tanoa at James's house for a grog session.

But more than anything, James like to throw a party. The wildest parties we ever had were at James's house, both in Savusavu and later in Sigatoka. He would go all out for these parties, have plenty of food, booze, loud music for dancing, and girls. James's parties were notorious for good times and anyone lucky enough to attend a party at his house usually had a smashing good time.

In true Fijian tradition, James would usually begin his parties by arriving modestly inebriated. How he did this I will never know but he usually managed to sneak away, get tanked up somewhere, and then return to the house where the action was to be. It was kind of like the party couldn't begin until James arrived, stumbled through the doors and yelled, "Hey, you guys! Wow, I'm smashed!" On that cue, the party began in earnest, a mass of sweating swirling bodies rocking to the latest pop hits.

One of the funnier instances of this occurred in Savusavu when James arrived back at his house one evening about party time. He was smashed as usual and covered with mud. James explained, after stumbling through the door, that he had an accident. As he staggered down the road in town, looking for a taxi to bring him home, he fell into a drainage ditch. Covered with mud and happily drunk, he was able to crawl up and out of the ditch and made it on home.

Another time, another party, this time in Sigatoka. The town was having its annual Coral Festival and many of the town's leading citizens were walking in the parade or riding on floats. James, not to be left behind, put on one of his wife's dresses with makeup on his face, lipstick, and a crown of seashells. He looked like the Queen of Lau, except for his beard and obviously drunken condition as he paraded through the streets of Sigatoka. Later that evening back at his house where a party was in full swing, he continued to be the life of the party while encouraging everyone to dance and be merry.

Big James of course was married to Nuku, our adopted "Auntie." But he still enjoyed flirting with the girls. One such time revealed James at his best at feeding the girls a line. Dave, Charlie, and I were in Sigatoka on leave visiting James and Nuku. He had taken us to a local tourist hotel for an afternoon beer break.

Seated near our table were a couple of young beautiful Australian girls. James, friendly and outgoing as he was, struck up a conversation with one of the girls. They began talking about Fiji's history, scenery, etc.

James introduced us and explained that we were Peace Corps Volunteers. And then he said to the girls, "Yes, I am a Volunteer too." The three of us nearly fell off our chairs. But James continued, "Yeah, I just came in from six months in the bush. Man, it's been a long time since I've seen a town."

At this point we were astonished by James's obvious attempt to feed this girl a line. It seemed that he had singled one girl out for his come on. Surprisingly, this girl went along with it and they continued to talk of Fiji.

James asked, "Oh, have you been to the Yasawas yet?"

"No," the girl answered, "what is that?"

"Well," James began, "it's a group of islands just west of Viti Levu here. They're located west of the international airport at Nadi."

"Oh," she replied, "what is there to see on the Yasawas?"

"Well, there is a cave there with beautiful shiny stones. It is so bright inside you don't even need a light to see. You really should go visit them," James said, trying to sound convincing.

He and the girl continued their small talk and finally the girls left, totally impressed with Big James and his knowledge of the local country.

James turned to us and said, "Gee, you guys, if she goes to the Yasawas she's going to be disappointed."

"Why is that James?" Dave asked puzzled.

"Well," James replied, "I've never even been to the Yasawas myself and there is no cave there that I know of!"

We all cracked up. It was so typical of Big James and his tall tales and trying to feed somebody a line. He sure liked to have fun with people.

Big James Makasiale was a real character.

Almost in a mirror-like reflection of James's features was his wife, Nuku. "Aunt Nuku" as we came to know her was also in her early 30's. Like James, she was from the Lau Islands of Fiji and appeared more Polynesian than Melanesian. She was a most beautiful woman, matched with a most beautiful personality that combined curiosity, warmth, friendliness, and a vibrant sense of humor so typical of Fijian women.

Nuku, having no children of her own at the time, took us under her protective and motherly wing after we first arrived in Savusavu. With this came a comfortable place to stay with tons and tons of excellent food, probably the consistently best food we had during our whole stay in Fiji.

Nuku became our good friend and in those early days helped with details of language and customs. She always looked forward to having us come and stay in their home. Even after James and Nuku were transferred to Sigatoka, we were always welcomed to their home. In fact, our leave times were purposely planned so that we would always spend part of our vacations at their home.

James and Nuku thought enough of us to invite us to their home time after time. And likewise, these two people, our friends James and Nuku, were lasting friends throughout our service in Fiji.

The last time we saw James and Nuku was during our final leave in September 1969. We paid a final farewell visit to Sigatoka at that time as in December when we terminated from the Peace Corps and left Fiji, we were unable to see them again.

Savenaca Koroinivalu was the Field Officer/Buca Bay for the Fiji Department of Agriculture. He was middle-aged, stood 5'9", weighed about 175 lbs. He was a native of Kadavu Island, a fact of which he was quite proud, as most Fijians are of their home island.

Save (Sa'vay) for short, was an ex-Sergeant Major in the Fiji Military Forces. He carried the military bearing and strong will into his daily life. He was however a true Fijian with a typical love of life, a joke, and a good time. Save became my friend, co-worker, confidant, and is some ways, a father. He taught me much about the agriculture department to which we were both responsible, the country, customs, and the language. Because Save spoke very good English however, we often used that as our communication mode, especially during work situations.

There was so much that I shared with Save: many a tanoa of grog in my bure, a night of cards, good times in travelling throughout our area of Buca Bay, and many a cigarette break.

There were many interesting things that we did together. One time while visiting new development blocks on Kioa Island, the boat that brought us to Kioa failed to wait for us to return and left without us. There we were, stranded on Kioa, a couple of miles across Buca Bay from Tukavesi, our station, with no way to get back. Hearing that there was a motorboat down the coast that could take us back across the bay, we decided to try to catch that boat. To get there, we borrowed another boat, a bulky old fishing skiff about 20 feet long. I sat on the bow deck and with the short paddle tried to keep the boat heading in the right direction as we followed the coastline. Save used his paddle at the stern.

On an extremely hot afternoon such as it was, it was a real effort for the two of us to move that boat the three miles or so to where we had to go. Due to the island's coastal terrain, there was no foot trail to follow to where we needed to go, so we had no choice. Fortunately, it was a calm day and we followed the shoreline, mangrove swamps, and reefs. We laughed and joked about it later but always remembered the day we paddled the boat around Kioa.

Another example of Save's interest and devotion to duty, Fijian style, was the time just the two of us killed a whole bottle of scotch whiskey. Among the many times we shared a grog session or a bottle, this instance stands out above all others.

Fijians, of course, drink to get drunk. Pure and simple. And Save being the strong-willed person he is, disliked leaving a task incomplete. We had a bottle one night and got together in my bure for some drinking. I had in mind a couple of friendly social drinks before dinner but Save thought differently.

One drink led to another and another. Part way through the bottle, I began to feel pretty high. I meekly suggested that we finish our glasses and save the rest of the bottle for the next time. Save, astounded by the mere thought responded, "But John, we must finish the bottle. It is our duty!"

There was no arguing with that man when it came to fulfilling one's duty. For Sergeant Major Savenaca, duty called and there was only one way to answer: finish that bottle. We proceeded to get fantastically smashed. Sitting in my bure, which served as a sort of recreation room as well as sleeping quarters for me, we were oblivious to the rest of the world.

Old Sergeant Major Savenaca would not shirk his duty to God, to Queen, to Country, or to Bottle!

Marama Koroinivalu was tired of the bush. She had been raising a family of seven youngsters through a series of various posts held by her husband, Savenaca. Most of the posts had been in isolated bush country stations like Buca Bay. Before that it had been Taveuni and before that somewhere else.

Marama was a middle-aged, gentle natured Fijian woman. She was a native of Rewa, a chiefly province on Viti Levu. She was a victim of Save's job, that is, she was stuck up in the bush country of Vanua Levu and did not much like it. She accepted her fate with sanguine fatalism. Nonetheless, she longed for the city of Suva, its conveniences, and her own people and relatives.

She was tired of the boredom of the bush, the lack of conveniences, the dearth of facilities, the solitude, the lack of good food so often, and so many other things we faced in our daily lives in Buca Bay. Despite all this, she maintained the unalterable jovial sense of humor so typical of Fijian women.

When I first met Marama at Tukavesi, before I moved there, she hovered in the background trying to assess me from a distance. I am sure she was apprehensive with the idea of having a foreigner come to live on the station with them. After I did finally relocate to Tukavesi, it was Marama who led the way in welcoming me and making me feel at home.

With five youngsters to care for, and two others away at school, Marama hardly needed another body to care for. However, I was taken in and adopted by the entire family. Marama did the cooking, washed clothes, laughed, joked, and generally provided everything to make me feel comfortable.

Marama, though she spoke some English, preferred to speak Fijian with me and helped me to improve my language. She did stress however that I speak English with the kids to help them. The kids were Naomi 12, their daughter, and sons Peni 11, Bola 10, Jone 8, and Savenaca Jr. 6. The two older sons, Saula 17 and Inoke 15, were away at secondary schools on Viti Levu.

On my travels back and forth to Savusavu I would make it a point to bring back some fresh bread or some fresh meat, commodities that were non-existent in Buca Bay. Marama greatly appreciated, as did all the family, the little goodies I was able to bring back from town. To me it was only a small way to pay back for all that they did for me, as they never let me pay for general support of the family. More importantly, the few fresh food products I brought from town gave us a supplement to the often-monotonous diet of canned fish, canned meat, dalo, tavioka, etc.

I recall one time in fact when Save was gone for several days on a trip, there was not much to eat in the house. So, to supplement what we had, I walked up the road to where an Indian farmer lived. I purchased a dozen fresh eggs for about 50 cents which was expensive as eggs were scarce as well. At any rate, Marama fixed the eggs for all of us to enjoy. No meal ever tasted better.

Marama was a uniquely beautiful person who gave so much of herself, expecting nothing in return. She touched my life in a special way and made my life as a Volunteer so much more meaningful.

If anyone is capable of having a heart of gold, then surely it must be Filo. Filomena Merekaulolo, in her mid-30's, small and rotund, lived in Tukavesi.

When I first saw Filo, I had just moved to Tukavesi. She worked for Doctor Joe, the medical officer, as housekeeper. Filo was the epitome of the Fijian village woman. She was every part the gentle natured, obedient, humble person but had a very robust sense of humor and a smile as wide and bright as the Pacific Ocean itself.

I first met her the night I had gone to the clinic, located on the hill just above the agriculture station where I lived. I was looking for the doctor to introduce myself to him. He happened to be gone at the time and so I met Filo. It was the beginning of a close and immensely helpful relationship. Filo was destined to become my "auntie," close friend, and cultural mentor.

Over the next year and a half of my residence in Tukavesi, I learned a great deal about Fijian culture and language from Filo. She spoke some English but told me she would only speak Fijian with me to help me improve. This she did and coupled with the other folks around me, I progressed rapidly in acquiring skill in the language.

Filo and Marama were the best of friends also and I established a wonderful relationship with both. Between the two of them, they managed to keep me laughing and joking about all kinds of things. Those two together personified the Fijian sense of humor.

But if one person taught me the beauty of the Fijian people, it was Filo. She had a generous loving heart and a soul of pure love for others. She helped me in so many ways that it is impossible to recall them all. Mostly though, she was simply my friend.

A journal entry for November 5, 1969, one month prior to my departure from Tukavesi, describes what I felt about Filo:

"I also went down to see Filo in the village. She made some masi for me and brought it up to me tonight. It is really beautiful masi, a real nice 'loloma' and souvenir of Fiji. I was hoping I would get some small pieces like she gave me. They are really nice.

Filo is a wonderful human being. She shows much warmth and love to everyone. She explained to me why she gave me the masi. God said to love all people, everywhere. And she realizes that my coming to Fiji was a great sacrifice for me personally. Being away from my family for so long, etc. So, she feels that by giving me a small gift, she can in a way help to make up for what I have sacrificed. She explained it all to me in Fijian and I understood all of it. It was beautiful."

For me personally, Filo is my most unforgettable character of Fiji. She symbolizes the greatest hope and expectations that a Peace

Corps Volunteer can have of touching someone else's life. She certainly touched mine.

Where Filo represented the best of what the village Fijian woman was like, our friend Lolo represented the best of the educated, sophisticated, modern oriented Fijian woman. Yet she still maintained that traditional earthiness, simplicity, and humorous nature so typical of Fijian women.

Sister Lolohae Waqatabu was the head nurse at Savusavu Hospital during most of our service in Cakaudrove. She was a nurse, a sister, not to be confused with a nun.

We met Lolo one day on a bus, coming down from Natewa Bay to Savusavu. Charlie in fact was the first one to strike up a conversation. Charlie, of course, was never one to let a pretty face go without recognition and prided himself on being suave, debonair, and who knows what else. And of course, Lolohae was beautiful.

She was tall, about 5'9", in her late 20's, and had a regal look about her. She was originally from Viti Levu. She was a most attractive girl with a ready smile and a charming set of dimples and bright eyes. She was also very sexy.

At any rate, Charlie got the three of us invited to the nurses' quarters at the hospital for dinner and drinks. This was a weekend in late 1968 and we were still making ourselves known throughout Cakaudrove.

Lolo was entertaining a couple of visiting Australian nurses from Suva and thought that we three guys would be nice sophisticated company for her party. She thought her guests would enjoy a nice pleasant conversation with three educated young Americans. Boy, was she wrong.

We arrived at Lolo's place on time and proceeded with dinner and some pleasant conversation. Afterwards, we sat in the parlor making small talk and enjoying cocktails. Charlie was mixing the drinks and before we knew what was happening, he was pouring super strong drinks, it was getting hotter than hell, and the three of us started getting smashed and acting silly.

To Lolohae's utter astonishment, her evening of pleasant conversation and company turned into a disaster as the three of us, fortified with strong drink, began speaking Fijian, cracking jokes, and generally acting outrageously. The sophisticated city girls did not quite know what to make of the situation but neither did Lolohae. The poor girls hardly knew what was going on as we continued to speak Fijian and ignored them. We generally made fools of ourselves.

After drinking most of the booze and without a doubt ruining our reputation with Lolo, we left her place. It was the next day when we began to wonder if we had done the right thing or not. To our surprise we ran into Lolo that day and figured we were going to get a real raking over.

To our surprise, Lolo was not angry or upset at all. If anything, she was amused by our general "bush behavior" of the previous evening.

"Do you realize what you did last night?" Lolo scoffed at us.

"Yes Lolo. Gee, we're sorry about that," Charlie said apologizing.

"Those poor Suva girls were shocked by your manners and behavior," said Lolo. "Why you acted just like a bunch of village boys come to town for a big night."

"Yes, yes, we're really sorry about that. But, well, there was no music or dancing and what else could we do?" Dave said in defense.

"Well, you could have at least acted a little more civilized than what you did. Do you realize the impression you gave those people last night? And here you are, supposed to be Americans. Why, you are nothing but a bunch of Fijian bush boys," Lolo said amusingly. Well, we certainly got a good scolding.

For us, it was the beginning of a beautiful friendship. We in time became good friends with Lolo and she was amused by our antics and very Fijianized behavior. Lolo forgave us our indiscretions for that first party at her place and was interested enough in us to invite us to several parties afterward. In fact, after our friend Big James left Savusavu, we had no parties to attend until Lolo happened on the scene. From there on we took part in some wild affairs, even for Savusavu.

One such party was held up at Savusavu government school which was just outside of town. One weekend when the three of us happened to be in town together, we called on Lolo to find that she had gone to a party at the school. We learned that several of the nurses, most of whom knew us by now, had also gone to this party. Some of the school-teachers had put together the party and invited the nurses.

We, of course, were not invited. But we did not let that little detail hamper us. It was a Saturday night and we were looking for some action. So, we got a taxi and rode out to the school where we proceeded to crash that party.

The nurses, the teachers, and everyone else at that gathering were stunned when we came barging in the building where the party was being held. We, of course, in true Fijian style, had a few beers under our belts. We could not enter a party completely sober.

When we arrived, everyone was sitting down making small talk with a record player turned on low. When we busted into that place, within a short time everyone was up dancing, moving around, and having a good time. We successfully and without a doubt added life to that party. Again, Lolo was amazed by our sheer gutsy approach. We enjoyed having a good time and everyone knew it.

Lolo remained our steadfast friend in Savusavu. We looked forward to going to Savusavu and spending some time with her, either at the movies, rugby games, a party, or just socializing at her place. She was a good friend who thought a lot of us and in what we were doing in our roles as Peace Corps Volunteers.

Our last few months in Cakaudrove were a little less enjoyable because Lolo was transferred to Sigatoka on Viti Levu where our other friends were. We were however able to see her a few times when we visited Sigatoka during our leave times.

If there was a word to describe Lolo, it would have to be class. She had plenty of that and was a person whom one could respect, admire, and love. She was truly an unforgettable character of Fiji.

To be called a "white Fijian" is probably the biggest compliment that could be bestowed on a foreigner living in Fiji. To be labeled a "white Fijian" necessarily implies that you have been in Fiji a long time, so long in fact that you have become Fijian. This is especially true for those foreigners living out in the bush country.

Father Ramon Jarre, a Frenchman by birth, was a "white Fijian" and yet one of the most respected and admired figures in Buca Bay. Father Jarre had been in Fiji for many years, serving the Catholic Church in numerous missions throughout the islands. When I first met him, he was the pastor of Napuka Catholic Mission on the northern peninsula tip of the Buca Bay area.

During the course of my travels for my work, I had several occasions to visit Napuka. I was always welcomed warmly by the good father. I always found a place to stay in Father's house and a hearty meal that was a welcome change from the all too often routine village food.

Father Ramon, in his late 50's, was a small man, 5'6", with a ruddy wrinkled complexion and wore the thickest pair of "coke bottle" glasses ever made. They apparently were heavy for he always used a safety strap to keep them on his head. Father spoke incredible Fijian with an amusing combination of a British-French accent. Nonetheless, he had a rapport and relationship with the people of the area that was singularly solid.

But over and above this, Father held the coveted title of "white Fijian" for his other skills. Father was a consummate smoker of the strong Fijian twist tobacco. He rolled it into small cigars and puffed away compulsively. This stuff was not for the faint hearted. It was a deep dark brown in color with an equally compelling aroma. When it was being smoked, it nearly suffocated you. To the uninitiated, one puff on this tobacco sent you reeling into a retching coughing spasm. It was that bad.

Most Fijians consumed the stuff by peeling off a couple of leaves from the tobacco roll and rolling them in newspaper. This made a dainty long thin cigarette. Banana leaves were also used. Others, the real macho type guys like Father Jarre, smoked the stuff straight up.

Another very distinctive trait that endeared Father to his flock was his amazing ability around the yaqona bowl. The good Father could easily drink many Fijians under the table at their own grog sessions. Father was so Fijianized in fact, that he had to have grog every day, usually in the afternoon while just sitting on the veranda of the mission house watching the school kids play in the courtyard.

When drinking grog from the coconut shell bilo, it was good custom to make as much noise as possible. So, you did not just sip the pepper liquid gingerly, but you slurped and guzzled it with gusto. This pleased the Fijians to no end and Father Jarre was a notorious grog swiller, one of the best.

One time Father came down to Tukavesi to say Sunday Mass. He drove his own Land Rover and often traveled around the villages of Buca Bay saying Masses and visiting his flock. Usually it would be customary for the people to have tea and cakes or some nice meal prepared for such a visitor. But not for Father Jarre. They all knew what he wanted and expected: yaqona, and plenty of it. In fact, on this day as soon as Mass was over, I joined Father and several of the villagers for a good grog session that must have lasted the better part of the afternoon. It was a standard procedure to have the grog bowl ready when Father Jarre came visiting.

On my visits to Napuka, especially when I stayed overnight, I could count on some enjoyable socializing. Besides being the congenial host he was, I found Father Ramon to be very observant, intelligent, and interesting individual. He was a well-read man, interested in world affairs, which was surprising for someone living in such a remote area like Napuka. He avidly read Newsweek Magazine, newspapers, and other periodicals as he could. We had many an enjoyable conversation about current and world affairs, politics, and so on.

Father Ramon Jarre, the "white Fijian," was one of the old hands of South Pacific lore, a truly incredible and unforgettable character.

If there was such a thing as a "mad doctor" then Buca Bay had its own in the personable figure of Dr. Joe Romanu. "Doc" had won his title, "Vuniwai Lialia," literally translated as "mad doctor," for his notorious and wild escapades.

Doc was 26 years old, stood 5'10", weighed 180 lbs., short hair on a muscular frame, and wore scholarly looking horn-rimmed glasses. A native of Kadavu, he was a graduate of the Fiji School of Medicine. While not the same as an M.D., he was trained as a medical practitioner to help meet the needs of the local people. He was the Medical Officer for Buca Bay in charge of the clinic at Tukavesi.

Doc spoke excellent English with a strong British accent. His favorite saying upon seeing a friend was, "Hey you bugger!" He was a friendly, outgoing person with an effervescent personality.

The Medical Department had given Doc a vehicle to drive on his rounds in Buca Bay. It was a small dune buggy thing called a Mini-moke. It had a collapsible canvas top; the trouble was that Doc had it so infrequently because it was usually being repaired. Doc kept running into coconut trees or into ditches. In fact, he really could not drive a motor vehicle.

When he was given the car, he had never driven before, like so many Fijians. Doc, being a macho guy, threw caution to the wind and drove like a mad man. He literally burned up the gravel roads around Buca Bay. As he roared through the villages and along the coast, all you could see was a cloud of dust. He fishtailed around curves, narrowly missing trees, ditches, drop offs, and the ocean. Doc became a different person once he got behind the wheel.

And that was why his little car ended up in the repair shop so often. Doc could not control the beast that was in him when he got behind the wheel. Inevitably, he ran into something. Luckily, he was never injured, not even his pride. For as soon as he got his wheels back, he would be out tearing up the roads again. He just never learned.

Doc had his troubles alright. He was such a wild driver that the police finally took away his driver's license for a while to teach him a lesson. And one other time, the medical department took away the car, thinking that doing without it might teach Doc a thing or two. Wrong. Neither action seemed to have much of an effect.

But Doc was a real good friend. There were many times that he invited me up to his house, just above where I lived in Tukavesi. We would often have lunch or dinner together. Other times we would have a grog session at night, play some cards, and listen to the radio or play some records on his battery powered record player. We would even have some of the sweet young things up from the village for dances that lasted till the early morning hours. Doc loved to have people around and enjoyed having a good time in true Fijian tradition.

One time in fact, Doc got into the beer brewing business. It was during the pineapple season when he began experimenting with making pineapple beer. He would use the medical clinic to sterilize bottles and prepare his mixture of pineapple pulp, sugar, yeast, and so on. He let the stuff ferment in the bottles for a couple of weeks or so.

The results were rather astonishing. The pineapple beer he made was great stuff. It was potent too and we spent a couple of nights up at Doc's place getting high on pineapple beer.

As all good things come to an end, Doc was eventually transferred to Viti Levu in mid-1969. So, I lost another good buddy, a guy who probably because of his notoriety, was transferred to the middle of Viti Levu where there were no roads and no medical department cars to smash up.

Dr. Joe Romanu was truly one of those unforgettable characters of Fiji who made my entire experience a little richer, a lot more colorful, and much more meaningful.

CHAPTER 15

THE GRAND ADVENTURE: A LOOK BACK

At the end, Dave, Charlie, and I were quite proud of ourselves. I mean of the dozen or so guys in agriculture related jobs in the Peace Corps Fiji I program, we were among the very few who served out the entire two years at our original assignments.

Several Volunteers from the Fiji II program had arrived in Cakaudrove in early 1969. These folks were assigned to various medical, co-operative, and teaching assignments throughout the province. Before the end of the year, all of them, except for one guy, had quit the province and transferred to other more desirable locations in Fiji, most notably near Suva. Cakaudrove had earned its reputation as a tough assignment for a Volunteer.

In early December 1969, each of us made our farewells to those with whom we lived. In my own case up at Tukavesi, Savenaca and Marama along with Filo, and many others, gave me a farewell party. I was presented with mats, a basket, and other souvenirs of my stay in Buca Bay.

It was hard to part with such beautiful loving people with whom I had become so close.

The agriculture department staff gave us a farewell party at the Wainigata Cocoa Station. It was a sad sweet affair at the same time. It was hard to believe that our service was over and yet too, we were happy to be moving on to other things.

In appreciation for our service over the two years, the staff presented "tabuas" to us. A tabua is a whale's tooth. In Fijian culture, it is a symbol of respect and honor, the highest acknowledgement one could expect to receive. With full and grateful hearts, Charlie, Dave, and I expressed our sincere thanks and best wishes to the agriculture staff of Savusavu. We had shared many experiences with these people over the two years of service.

On December 5, 1969, Dave and I boarded a Fiji Airways flight at Savusavu Airport bound for Suva. Charlie would attend to last minute errands in Savusavu and would join up with us in Suva the next day.

As the four engine Heron roared down the gravel airstrip, a swath cut through towering coconut trees, Dave and I looked at each other. A few tears even welled up in our eyes.

"Dave, put it there partner," I said extending my hand across the aisle.

"John, we did it man! We spent two years in Cakaudrove," Dave exclaimed.

"Congratulations buddy!" I said as we shook hands.

"We can be damned proud of what we did," Dave replied.

As we glanced out the windows, the plane lifted and soared into the bright Fijian sky. Below, the airstrip was soon swallowed up by the coconut groves that stretched along the coast of Vanua Levu. The deep blue ocean lapped at the reef fringed shores of Cakaudrove. As the plane turned south and headed for Suva, the green hills and blue lagoons faded behind us.

On December 8, 1969, we were officially terminated from the Peace Corps in Suva. We were now "civilians" again and free to do what we wanted. Of the original fifty-six Fiji I Volunteers, only forty-seven completed the full two years of service. Of these, only a handful asked for an extension of service. The rest, like us, terminated and set off on their own.

Like most too, we were in no hurry to return to the United States and home. We wanted to see a little bit more of the world first. Dave, Charlie, and I had planned out a trip that would take us around the Pacific Basin before our return to the States. We left Fiji within a couple of days for New Zealand, and from there to Australia, Southeast Asia, and the Far East. We spent the next several weeks travelling before we finally arrived back in the States and our homes.

And so, one can ask, what did we accomplish in Fiji? What is the sum of our two years there? To be frank, that is not an easy question to answer.

If one looked for concrete results and examples of our achievements there, he would find few, if any. The Peace Corps experience is such that it cannot often be measured or evaluated based on observed improvements or results. At least this was the case with our situation in Cakaudrove.

It has been many years now, since the experience, a lifetime ago. Perhaps too, time has a way of mellowing the experience. Still then, looking back, the experience was gratifying. It was a profound influence on our lives, each in his own way. We gained immensely from it, we grew, and we matured.

I have no doubt that it affected my own personal attitudes and values. I have often wondered just what my life would be like had I not had the experience. I shudder to think about it.

Essentially, the Peace Corps experience in Fiji was a human experience exploring the human condition. Perhaps if nothing substantial came out of it, it was at least an experience in understanding and sharing between people of different cultures. In my estimation, it was an invaluable experience. It could not be measured in time or money alone. It was much more than that.

In summing up the experience, I recall that Dave once said, "You know John, I always wanted to live in a humanistic society, a society where people share their lives with each other. I finally got that chance here in Fiji and I'm glad I did. It's been a hell of an experience."

And Charlie too, succinctly summed it up like this. "I feel good about my time in Fiji," he explained, "because I have known some very good people there."

And that is pretty much what the experience boiled down to in the end: the people. It was the type of grand adventure that helped us to better understand people, our fellow man, and perhaps even to better understand ourselves. Sometimes that is enough.

The following passages are taken from some of the final journal writings from November 1969, as I finished up my final days at Buca Bay. At times, the passages reveal the bittersweet feelings I held at the time regarding the situation and the broader feelings I held toward the overall experience. Looking at these passages in retrospect, the ideas expressed still seem appropriate.

November 1969, Buca Bay, Vanua Levu, Fiji:

"...A lot has been written and said about the South Pacific, its people, culture, and so on. I've read quite a lot about it, but I've sure as hell experienced much more as a Peace Corps Volunteer living here for two years. I've talked and discussed and analyzed just about every aspect of living here with my fellow Volunteers. There's hardly an angle we've not covered.

...I've personally tried to analyze the experience as per my role as a Volunteer and what I've done, or contributed to Fiji, and what Fiji has done to me. It's a complex thing ...I've still got another month to go before I leave Fiji, but I feel that many of my feelings about the place and my experience are already concrete.

...As I look back to the early weeks and months of my stay here in Fiji, I really wonder how I even stuck it out. I guess I was just curious and had a will to try, and a great desire to just 'stick it out' come what may. Then the first year or so I had a definite job to do, though this came about gradually.

...I think that overall, I have thoroughly enjoyed my two years here in Fiji. It has been a totally different experience, one that I couldn't have gotten any other way. It's been a very maturing and educational experience for me.

...True, I've gotten sick and tired of the eternal sameness of everything around me. The same food every day, the same roads, the same houses, hills, music on the radio, etc. But the people are what have changed me. They are the significant factor in changing my attitudes in general.

...I must recognize my indebtedness to these wonderful Fijian people who have contributed so much to my experience here. Yes, I am fed up with the diet, cold baths, muddy roads, and a thousand and one other things...but these material things are of less value and importance than the value of human relationships such as I have here established with these people.

...These past few months I feel have been perhaps the most difficult to go through. I have had very little to occupy my time, work wise, and this has been very difficult to bear. There is perhaps nothing more boring, dull, and nerve wracking than trying to busy yourself from day to day.

...There is also another thing which has a great influence upon my day to day morale also. That is loneliness. I do feel very lonely sometimes, even though I am surrounded by Fijian friends. I have had a tremendous friendship here in Fiji with two fellow Volunteers, Dave, and

Charlie. They have meant very much to me, to my morale. When I spend a week or two here at my station...I have a great desire to be with them...

...There's really no one else to talk with up here where I am at. You are really all on your own, and if you can't adjust to the loneliness, to being by yourself...then you wouldn't be able to stick it out for very long.

...Tonight, after supper, a simple meal of fish, greens, and breadfruit, I played cards and listened to the radio, Radio Tonga, with Save here at the station. Marama and the kids slept early, as usual. It was a breezy evening, giving hints of further rain such as we had today. I was listening to the nice Tongan music over the radio and thought how much island music, the sounds of the South Pacific, really is beautiful.

...These moments like this tonight, I enjoy them and they are perhaps the best part of my visit to this place called Fiji. I have thoroughly enjoyed so many of the pleasant times like these, just relaxing and listening to the music...I will miss times like these.

...I was thinking today as I lay in my house doing nothing but existing, of the Peace Corps ad I saw on TV long ago. It showed a college age guy playing cards by himself and said, 'If you've got nothing to do, why don't you join the Peace Corps and do something for the world?' or something to that effect.

...I just thought, 'Boy, if Peace Corps/Washington big shots could just see me right now, wouldn't they be in for a shock.' Because here I was 7000 miles 'out in the field' not doing a damned thing!"

In the final analysis, the Peace Corps experience in Fiji or in any other country for that matter is a purely individual one. It is simply a people to people program of international brotherhood, goodwill and understanding. For those curious enough to explore and learn about the world and about themselves, it is without a doubt, the grand adventure.

THE END

EPILOGUE

*I*n the years since their shared experiences in Fiji, the "Cakaudrove Team" members have gone their separate ways and reunions have not been as frequent as they would like. However, the positive feelings for their common experiences in Fiji have continued to keep them in touch with each other over the years.

Charles Matthews and his wife, Joan, live in North Aurora, Illinois. After returning from Fiji, Charles completed an M.S. degree in counseling at Roosevelt University in Chicago and spent his working career as a mental health counselor and director of a mental health clinic in Chicago. In addition, he has also served as an elder and later as pastor at Trinity Chapel Church in Batavia, Illinois, the church founded by his father.

Dave Reed and his wife, Jeanne, live in rural Trilla, Illinois. After returning from Fiji, Dave completed an M.S. degree in social work at Catholic University in Washington, D.C. He worked in Illinois as a child abuse social worker and in the Veterans Administration Hospital in Danville. He also served a hitch in the U.S. Army and spent several years in the Army Reserve. Still serving, he is on the board of directors of the Human Rights Authority of the Illinois Guardianship and Advocacy Commission which assesses cases of abuse/neglect of disabled people.

John Penisten and his wife, Susan, live in Hilo, Hawai`i, but also spend lots of time visiting family in Minnesota. After returning from Fiji, John completed an M.S. in education at Drake University, taught briefly in Ames, Iowa, public schools and then moved to Hawai'i. He joined the faculty of Hawai`i Community College in Hilo, teaching literacy and college survival skills courses. He retired after over 30 years in education.